Learning Modular Java Programming

Explore the power of modular programming for building applications with Java and Spring!

Tejaswini Mandar Jog

BIRMINGHAM - MUMBAI

Learning Modular Java Programming

First published: June 2016

Production reference: 1270616

Published by Packt Publishing Ltd.
Livery Place
35 Livery Street
Birmingham B3 2PB, UK.

ISBN 978-1-78588-882-3

www.packtpub.com

Credits

Author
Tejaswini Mandar Jog

Reviewer
Dionisios Petrakopoulos

Acquisition Editor
Larissa Pinto

Content Development Editor
Shali Deeraj

Technical Editor
Anushree Arun Tendulkar

Copy Editor
Safis Editing

Project Coordinator
Sanchita Mandal

Proofreader
Safis Editing

Indexer
Monica Ajmera Mehta

Graphics
Jason Monteiro

Production Coordinator
Aparna Bhagat

Cover Work
Aparna Bhagat

About the Author

Tejaswini Mandar Jog is a passionate and enthusiastic SCJP-certified trainer. She has more than eight years' experience in the IT training field, specializing in Java, J2EE, and relevant technologies. She has worked with many renowned corporate companies on training and skill enhancement programs. She is also involved in the development of projects using Java, Spring, and Hibernate.

I still remember the very first conversation with the editor about the book. Before that day I was just a reader, I never thought of writing a book. But now I had an opportunity to be an author! I was in a dilemma, and confused—can I be? But then my personal guide and philosopher Mandar gave me the confidence to go for it. Thank you Mandar not just for providing strong support, but also for your valuable suggestions, which helped me to improve the contents.

This book would not have been completed without the help of Shali, the editor. Her suggestions and efforts made the difference. Aaron, the acquisition editor, thank you for showing confidence in me, and giving me the confidence to write this book.

Without the best wishes and support of my family, it is doubtful that I would have completed this book.

It would be mean of me not to mention Ojas, my lovely son. I really appreciate the way he supported me, so that I was able to write peacefully. Love you a lot dear!!!

Finally, thank you to all who helped by supporting me directly and indirectly to complete this book. Thank you all just for being with me!!!

About the Reviewer

Dionisios Petrakopoulos has worked in several companies, using different programming languages (C, C++, Java SE, Java EE, and Scala) and technologies, as a senior software engineer for the past 15 years. His main interest is the Java ecosystem and the various facets of it. His other area of interest is information security, and especially cryptography. He holds a BSc in computer science and an MSc in information security, both from Royal Holloway, University of London.

I would like to thank my wife, Anna, for her support and love.

www.PacktPub.com

eBooks, discount offers, and more

Did you know that Packt offers eBook versions of every book published, with PDF and ePub files available? You can upgrade to the eBook version at www.PacktPub. com and as a print book customer, you are entitled to a discount on the eBook copy. Get in touch with us at customercare@packtpub.com for more details.

At www.PacktPub.com, you can also read a collection of free technical articles, sign up for a range of free newsletters and receive exclusive discounts and offers on Packt books and eBooks.

https://www2.packtpub.com/books/subscription/packtlib

Do you need instant solutions to your IT questions? PacktLib is Packt's online digital book library. Here, you can search, access, and read Packt's entire library of books.

Why subscribe?

- Fully searchable across every book published by Packt
- Copy and paste, print, and bookmark content
- On demand and accessible via a web browser

Instant updates on new Packt books

Get notified! Find out when new books are published by following @PacktEnterprise on Twitter or the *Packt Enterprise* Facebook page.

Table of Contents

Preface   v

Chapter 1: Introducing Modular Programming   1

  Software – the perspective   1
  Modules   3
    What is behind and in a module?   3
      The practical aspect   3
  The gang – modular programming   4
    The world of modules   4
  Tiers and layers in an enterprise application   5
    One-tier applications   7
    Two-tier applications   7
    Three-tier applications   8
    N-tier applications   9
    Java Enterprise architecture   11
  Sharing the work   12
  Coordinate with the team   13
    Versioning tools   13
      Centralized versioning   14
      The architecture of SVN   15
      Distributed versioning   17
  Summary   17

Chapter 2: Saying Hello to Java EE   19

  The enterprise as an application   19
  The Java EE platform   20
    Features of the Java EE platform   21
    The world of dotcoms   22
    Servlet – the dynamicity   23
    MVC I architecture   24
    MVC II architecture   25

The practical aspect	25
What is a framework?	29
Spring MVC	30
The components	31
The front controller	32
Spring MVC controller	32
ModelAndView	32
ViewResolver	33
The configuration file	33
Summary	39
Chapter 3: Implementing the Presentation Layer	**41**
Presentation	**41**
Data binding	43
Case 1 – Reading request parameters for searching	43
Case 2 – Reading multiple form fields	46
Form validation	53
Developing customized validators using Spring validators	54
Annotation-based validations	59
Summary	**65**
Chapter 4: Talking to the Database	**67**
Persistence	**67**
Using object serialization	68
Disadvantages of using object serialization	68
Storing data in XML	68
Disadvantages of storing data in XML	68
Saving the data in a relational database	68
Advantages of saving data in a relational database	69
Interaction of Java with relational databases	**69**
Types of JDBC drivers	70
JDBC-ODBC bridge driver	70
JDBC Native API Driver/Partly Java Driver	71
JDBC Net Protocol Driver	72
All Java drivers	73
Spring-JDBC integration	76
Configuring DataSource in Spring JDBC	77
Types of integration of JDBC	78
Integrating the DataSource to get a connection reference	79
Integrating the JDBC template	82
Integrating JDBC DAO support	84
Problems with JDBC	86
Introduction to ORM	**86**
Advantages of using ORM	86
Introduction to Hibernate	86
Hibernate architecture	87

Spring Hibernate integration   93
Introduction to unit testing   **98**
Unit testing using JUnit   98
Steps for writing a TestCase using annotation   98
Summary   **102**
Chapter 5: Developing the Business Layer   **103**
Business logic   **104**
Domain knowledge   106
Rules, formulas, and conditions   107
Case studies   107
Developing the business layer   107
Transaction management   **111**
JDBC and transaction management   112
Spring and transaction management   112
Programmatic transaction   113
Declarative transaction   113
Declarative transaction management   117
Programmatic transaction management   119
Summary   **121**
Chapter 6: Testing Your Application   **123**
Software testing   **123**
The waterfall model   124
The spiral model   125
The V model   125
Verification phases   126
Validation phases   126
Mock testing   **127**
Spring testing framework   127
Case1 – Inserting contact with correct values as per validation rules 128
Case2 – Inserting a contact by violating validation rules for contacts 130
Why integration testing?   **133**
Mockito testing   **141**
Arquillian   146
Summary   **147**
Chapter 7: Securing the Application   **149**
Make it safe, make it secure   **149**
Spring security framework   **151**
Secure web request   152
Way 1 – Spring Security for URL using servlet filters   153
Case 1 – Basic authentication   157
Case 2 – Login form authentication   161
Case 3 – Authentication against database   163

Case 4 – Remember me	165
Case 5 – Logout	167
Way 2 – Spring Security using AOP	168
@Secured	168
@RolesAllowed	168
SpEL-enabled security annotations for securing the methods	169
Spring Security using pointcut	171
Way 3 – Custom security	172
Summary	**172**
Chapter 8: Versioning and Deploying	**173**
Versioning	**173**
Collabnet server	174
Visual SVN server	**180**
Adding SVN as a plugin to Eclipse	188
Adding files in the project and committing them to the repository	193
Importing the project in the workspace	194
Updating and tracking the project for latest changes in the repository	196
Project deployment	**198**
Copying a WAR file into Tomcat without Tomcat manager	198
Copying a WAR file into Tomcat with Tomcat manager	201
Summary	**203**
Index	**205**

Preface

Welcome to the world of Java EE development! A huge world, with a large number of things to learn and so many skills to adapt. It's actually difficult to decide what to start with. When I started, I faced a similar problem. Now, also when I am in training sessions or seminars, I find many people who want be professional developers, but don't have much exposure to the processes, stages, and thinking involved in application development. This book helps you by providing a path for web development that can used to understand the process of Java modular development through an easy-to-understand case study. Nowadays, in Java EE, there are many technologies in the market. One such technology is Spring.

Spring is useful for developing independent Java modules that can then be combined to create a complete application. We have used Spring, Spring MVC, and many of its features throughout the book, while discussing the concepts of database, unit testing, security, and many other topics.

What this book covers

Chapter 1, *Introducing Modular Programming*, starts with a discussion about Enterprise application, its architecture, and its development. Enterprise application development is a team that activity faces many problems concerning collaboration between team members. We will introduce coordinated development and the tools involved in this chapter.

Chapter 2, *Saying Hello to Java EE*, involves a short warm up by discussing and developing a Java web application using Servlet-JSP. We will redevelop the application using a Spring to get startup gear as Spring MVC developer.

Chapter 3, *Implementing the Presentation Layer*, discusses the points that need to be taken care of when developing the most important layer of an application: the presentation layer. We will discuss how to develop the pages to incorporate data binding for business logic, as well as for presentation, using Spring MVC features.

Chapter 4, *Talking to the Database*, discusses Spring JDBC connectivity. Data collected from the user and data to be used in the business logic need to be persisted. We will also cover Spring DAO support persistency. We will then move on a step and introduce Hibernate, the ORM technology, and its integration with Spring. We will also cover unit testing to make sure our code is working fine.

Chapter 5, *Developing the Business Layer*, discusses the development of the most important layer of an application—the business layer—and the communication between the layers. An application needs to be developed by following a number of business rules.

Chapter 6, *Testing Your Application*, explains that the modules developed by the developer should produce the correct result. To ensure the correctness of the code in this chapter, we will cover the basics of testing with the help of the V module. We will also cover integration testing with JUnit and Mockito.

Chapter 7, *Securing the Application*, discusses why and how to secure the application. In an application, there are certain modules that are open and available to all, and some that are restricted. We will apply the Spring security module to secure the Spring MVC application with the help of basic and form based security.

Chapter 8, *Versioning and Deploying*, shows us how to collaborate on the application, which has been developed in parts, or by different team members simultaneously. In this chapter, we will set up and integrate Tortoise SVN as a versioning tool used to collaborate on the code. We will also discuss the creation of repositories, users, and setting access rules for Collabnet and Visual SVN servers.

What you need for this book

You will need to have sound knowledge and practical exposure of core Java to understand this book. Along with this, knowledge of basic JDBC and the concepts of object-oriented programming language is required. As we are using Eclipse IDE throughout the book, you should be familiar with it. Those who have an introductory knowledge of Spring beginner framework can refer to this book easily. If you are beginner for Spring, we suggest you first go through the basic concepts of Spring configuration and get some practical experience. A basic knowledge of Hibernate and JUnit will be an added advantage.

Who this book is for

The idea for this book is to give the reader experience of creating an application step by step using Java modular programming step by step. The book is useful for any novice developer who wants to get exposure of modular Java development. The book is also useful for anyone who wants to have a roadmap for developing an application in stages such as problem statement, UI development, business logic development, database layer development, and so on. The book covers all the aspects of application development required into a turn a the problem statement to product, with coverage of security, maintaining versions, and the deployment process.

Conventions

In this book, you will find a number of text styles that distinguish between different kinds of information. Here are some examples of these styles and an explanation of their meaning.

Code words in text, database table names, folder names, filenames, file extensions, pathnames, dummy URLs, user input, and Twitter handles are shown as follows: "Every object created based on this type will inherit these default properties such as `toString`, `valueOf`, `hasOwnProperty`, and so on."

A block of code is set as follows:

```
function doAddition(num1, num2){
   return num1 + num2;
}
function doSubtraction(num1, num2){
   var result = null;
   if(num1 > num2){
   result = num1 - num2;

   }else{
      result = num2 - num1;
   }
   return result;
}
```

 Warnings or important notes appear in a box like this.

 Tips and tricks appear like this.

Reader feedback

Feedback from our readers is always welcome. Let us know what you think about this book — what you liked or disliked. Reader feedback is important for us as it helps us develop titles that you will really get the most out of.

To send us general feedback, simply e-mail feedback@packtpub.com, and mention the book's title in the subject of your message.

If there is a topic that you have expertise in and you are interested in either writing or contributing to a book, see our author guide at www.packtpub.com/authors.

Customer support

Now that you are the proud owner of a Packt book, we have a number of things to help you to get the most from your purchase.

Downloading the example code

You can download the example code files for this book from your account at http://www.packtpub.com. If you purchased this book elsewhere, you can visit http://www.packtpub.com/support and register to have the files e-mailed directly to you.

You can download the code files by following these steps:

1. Log in or register to our website using your e-mail address and password.
2. Hover the mouse pointer on the **SUPPORT** tab at the top.
3. Click on **Code Downloads & Errata**.
4. Enter the name of the book in the **Search** box.
5. Select the book for which you're looking to download the code files.
6. Choose from the drop-down menu where you purchased this book from.
7. Click on **Code Download**.

You can also download the code files by clicking on the **Code Files** button on the book's webpage at the Packt Publishing website. This page can be accessed by entering the book's name in the **Search** box. Please note that you need to be logged in to your Packt account.

Once the file is downloaded, please make sure that you unzip or extract the folder using the latest version of:

- WinRAR / 7-Zip for Windows
- Zipeg / iZip / UnRarX for Mac
- 7-Zip / PeaZip for Linux

The code bundle for the book is also hosted on GitHub at `https://github.com/PacktPublishing/Learning-Modular-Java-Programming`. We also have other code bundles from our rich catalog of books and videos available at `https://github.com/PacktPublishing/`. Check them out!

Errata

Although we have taken every care to ensure the accuracy of our content, mistakes do happen. If you find a mistake in one of our books—maybe a mistake in the text or the code—we would be grateful if you could report this to us. By doing so, you can save other readers from frustration and help us improve subsequent versions of this book. If you find any errata, please report them by visiting `http://www.packtpub.com/submit-errata`, selecting your book, clicking on the **Errata Submission Form** link, and entering the details of your errata. Once your errata are verified, your submission will be accepted and the errata will be uploaded to our website or added to any list of existing errata under the Errata section of that title.

To view the previously submitted errata, go to `https://www.packtpub.com/books/content/support` and enter the name of the book in the search field. The required information will appear under the **Errata** section.

Piracy

Piracy of copyrighted material on the Internet is an ongoing problem across all media. At Packt, we take the protection of our copyright and licenses very seriously. If you come across any illegal copies of our works in any form on the Internet, please provide us with the location address or website name immediately so that we can pursue a remedy.

Please contact us at `copyright@packtpub.com` with a link to the suspected pirated material.

We appreciate your help in protecting our authors and our ability to bring you valuable content.

Questions

If you have a problem with any aspect of this book, you can contact us at questions@packtpub.com, and we will do our best to address the problem.

1
Introducing Modular Programming

Software development is a complex, time-consuming process, where success depends on teamwork. We keep on talking about software or software development. Sometimes we are part of the process as well. But we will be in one of the roles as architect, developer, tester, or deployer. Though we are always concentrating on a role, knowing the overall process always benefits us.

In this chapter, we will be going through the following topics:

- What is software and software development?
- What are enterprise applications?
- The role of modular programming in enterprise applications
- Introduction to and the importance of versioning

Software – the perspective

A software application is a program which enables end users to perform a specific task, for example, online money transfer, and withdrawal of money from an ATM or the use of an Eclipse to develop an application. This application is complex, scalable, and distributed, providing a complete solution to the end user. Applications known as enterprise applications are needs-based, providing solutions to business requirements rather than to an individual. The organization will use this application or integrate it within an existing application.

Enterprise applications may vary from business to business, for example, school or employee management systems, banking applications, online shopping applications, or e-commerce applications. All such enterprise applications provide displaying, processing, and storing data as their basic feature. Along with these features, the application can also provide transaction management and security services as advanced features. We access such applications typically through a network system rather than on an individual machine.

Let's briefly discuss the software development process before moving ahead:

- The software is always a solution or part of the solution to an enterprise problem. A good start in the development process is knowing exactly what the expectations are from the software, what types of solutions need to be included, what the data input will be, and what the output from the application is. This phase will be called the **requirement collection phase**.

- Once we get an idea about the requirements, now it's time to decide the hardware specification, the system requirements, the architecture to use, the design to follow, and so on. This phase is called **designing**.

- Using the design document, now developers will come in action to start a very important phase called **development**, where the actual coding takes place.

- Suppose we have developed a product; how do we prove that it is the right solution for the requirements which we got in the first phase? Yes, with the help of **testing**. We can carry out unit testing, integration testing, assembly testing, and acceptance testing to ensure that the requirement has been met.

- After successful testing, now it's time for the user to use it. This is nothing but the **deployment** phase, after which it is ready for use.

- Talking in terms of one phase after deployment, the work is over but what if any runtime issue emerges? What if the client recommends some minor or major changes? Or what if it has a bug? Because of this, post-deployment is also a very important step, which we call **maintenance**.

Although these phases theoretically come one after another, there can be different approaches called **software development process models**, such as the waterfall model, iterative model, spiral model, v model, agile model, and so on.

Modules

Application development is composed of many interconnected parts which interact with each other. To withstand high market demand and increasing competition, software should have a good look and feel, and ease of use. To develop a compatible solution, the developer has to think about compound structure as well as user perspective. It's quite difficult to develop such a product single-handed. It's teamwork, where the development is running alongside. The team members will build up separate small modules dedicated to part of the actual solution. These small modules will be clubbed together and interact with each other to form a complete solution.

What is behind and in a module?

Each module which has been developed will be performing a unique responsibility. When a module is responsible for a single task, it will be called **cohesive**. The cohesiveness will make the module more maintainable. Also, it will be less frequently changed. A good design perspective is to try writing a module which will be highly cohesive.

The two modules developed separately will now need to have interaction. To make them interactive, we have to introduce them. This will be done by making them dependent on each other. This dependency is termed **coupling**. When the code size and number of modules are small, coupling won't be a problem. But in an enterprise application, the code size is huge. Any little change makes a difference and then all of its dependencies should be changed accordingly at a number of places. This makes the code unmanageable. So it's always recommended to have loosely coupled modules.

The practical aspect

Let's take the example of a desktop, the one which we use in our routine. A desktop consists of a monitor, CPU, keyboard, and mouse. If a new monitor with some advanced features is introduced in the market, what we will do? Will we buy a new desktop or just replace the monitor?

As per the convenience and also the cost, it's feasible to just replace the monitor and not the whole desktop; how come this is possible? It's possible because the desktop is assembled with subunits, which are easily replaceable. Each subunit is cohesive for the work and they are not tightly coupled. This happens when we use modularization. When we write an application that uses similar concepts, it is called **modular programming**.

The gang – modular programming

Modular programming is the process of dividing a problem into smaller subunits and then making them interact with each other. Each subunit will revolve around a part of the problem. These subparts are quite easily reusable or replaceable. This designing technique gives a helping hand to the developers to develop their individual units and later combine them. Each subpart can be termed a module. The developers do not need to know what the other modules are or how they have been developed. Modularizing the problem will help the developers to achieve high cohesion.

The world of modules

The pluggable component which can be easily integrated into the application will provide the solution to a particular problem. For example, we want an Eclipse to support **Subversion (SVN)** (one of the versioning tools). Now, we have two choices. One, to start the development of Eclipse again from scratch or, two, to develop an SVN application. If we choose the first choice, it's very time-consuming and we already have Eclipse in a working condition. Then why start it from scratch? Yes, it's a very bad idea. But it would be great to have an SVN solution to be developed separately which is an SVN plugin; this plug-in can be easily integrated into eclipse. See how easily the two modules — eclipse, which was in working and the new SVN module — have been integrated. As SVN is a separate module, it can be integrated with NetBeans (one of the IDEs). If we had developed it in eclipse, then it would not be possible to integrate it in any other IDE. When we develop any application, from our point of view, it's always the best. But being a good developer, we need to be sure of it. How to check whether the application we have developed is working fine for the aspects or not? Yes, we need to test it, whether each part is working correctly or not. But is it really so simple? No, it's not. Not just because of complicated logic but due to its dependency. Dependency is a factor which is not under the control of the developer. For example, we need to check whether my credentials are correct or not when I am trying to login. We don't want to test the tables where the data is stored, but we want to check whether the logic of tracking the data is correct or not. As we have developed a separate data access module, the testing becomes easy. In Java, a single functionality can be tested with JUnit.

Testing helps the developer to test an application which processes the data and provides an output. If we are getting the correct result, we do not have a problem, but what if the output is wrong? The process of finding bugs in a module is called debugging. The debugging helps us to find defects in an application. That means we need to track the flow and then find out where the problem started. It's quite difficult to find the defect if the system is without modules or if the modules are tightly coupled. So it's good programming practice to write an application which consists of highly cohesive, loosely coupled modules.

There is one more fact which we need to discuss here. Sometimes, when the actual main development is progressing, we come across a point where we actually want to add a new feature. This new feature was not added while the basic discussion was going on; here, we want to do parallel development. In this case, we don't want to replace the previous development but we want to support or enhance it. As our application consists of modules, a developer can go ahead as most of these modules are independent and can be reused.

Tiers and layers in an enterprise application

An enterprise application is an application which has been developed to fulfill the requirements of a business. Being an enterprise application, it normally has huge code. Maintaining such huge code all together is a very complex task. Also, developing the code takes lots of time. So the code is been divided into small, maintainable modules which can be easily developed separately and later on combined to give a final product. All modules which provide similar kind of functionality will be grouped together to form a **layer**. These layers are the logical separation of modules. But sometimes, for better performance, one layer can be also spread over the network.

Layers are a logical separation of the code to increase maintainability. But when we physically move one typical layer and deploy it on another machine, then it will be called as a **tier**. At any one time, many users will be using the enterprise application simultaneously, so the use of a tiered application provides good performance.

Let's consider a web module for login. The user will open the browser and the login page will be rendered. The user will enter their credentials (username and password). After submitting the form, a request will be sent to the server to perform the authentication. Once the data is received on the server side, the business logic layer will process the data and put the result in the response. The result depends on whether the credentials are present in database or not.

Finally, the response will be generated and the result will be sent back to the browser. Here, the user interface, business logic, and database are the three distinct features involved. These are called as the presentation layer, business logic layer, and data storage layer, respectively.

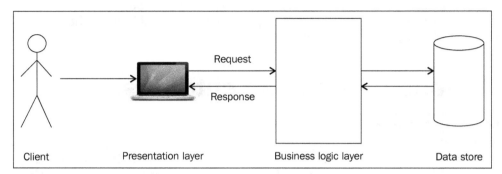

Layers in an enterprise application

Each of these layers will talk with the above layer and exchange data. The process broadly takes place as follows:

- The user will open the browser and hit the URL.
- A login page will be rendered on the browser. The user will fill in the form and submit it to be processed by the business logic layer.
- To check the data, the business logic layer will communicate with the data storage layer.
- According to the result returned from the data storage layer, the business logic layer will now send the result to the presentation layer and the client's browser will render the results page.

Now we understand the difference between a tier and a layer, let's discuss tiers in detail. Depending on how many physical separations one application is using, it will be called a one-tier, two-tier, or multi-tier application.

One-tier applications

An enterprise application where all the components reside on a single computer will be called as a one-tier application. These applications can also be called single-tier applications. So we can broadly say that these are the applications which get installed and run on a single computer.

For example, an Eclipse application as software. When we install eclipse and launch it, it will be running on our personal computer. It doesn't require any network. The presentation layer, that is, Swing GUI, business logic, and storing information in a filesystem will be done on the same computer.

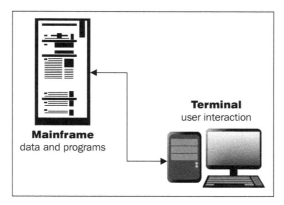

A one-tier application

Two-tier applications

When the enterprise application gets divided over two computers, it will be called a two-tier application. Generally the data storage, that is, the database, will be moved onto a separate, dedicated computer. This will work as a database host machine or database server. The presentation layer and business logic layer will be residing in one location and data layer will be residing in another.

An example of this is the Oracle database management system. When we want to use an Oracle database, we will install Oracle on a dedicated machine which can be called as the Oracle server. Now, on the user's machine, we can install the Oracle client. Whenever we want to fetch data from the table in Oracle, we will use the client application, which will connect to the server and give the required data.

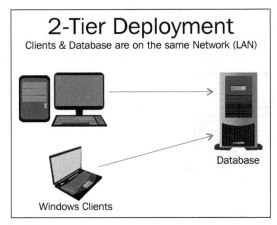

A two-tier application

Three-tier applications

When in an application, the presentation layer, business layer, and data layer will be running on their dedicated servers and interact with each other through a network, it will be called a **three-tier application**. The web server is dedicated to the presentation layer, the middleware server is dedicated to the business layer, and the database server is dedicated to the database layer. The middleware server can also provide services such as transaction and connection polling.

For example, any online shopping application can be considered a three-tier application. Let's see how. In this application, the products will be displayed on a browser in presentation pages. The business logic part, such as the calculation of discounts, the total amount which the buyer has to pay, and so on, using transaction or messaging services, will be provided by the application server. The buyer's information, product information, bank details, delivery address, and so on, will be saved in the tables on the database server for further reference. That means the presentation tier, application tier and data tier are the three tiers which play roles in this application.

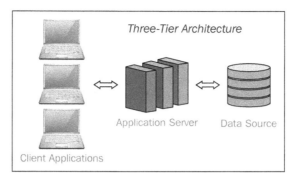

A three-tier application

N-tier applications

With the increase in the use of the Internet, it's very important for an application to be capable of serving many requests at the same time. This puts a burden on the server. In terms of performance, it's a better solution to take away the presentation layer from the business logic and deploy it separately. It can be deployed on one dedicated web server or may be on different servers. In the same way, the business logic and database layers can be separated on different servers partially or completely residing in one or more machines.

The client tier, presentation tier, business tier, and database tier are separated on separate machines. They interact with each other through a network and perform their services. This will be called an **N-tier application**.

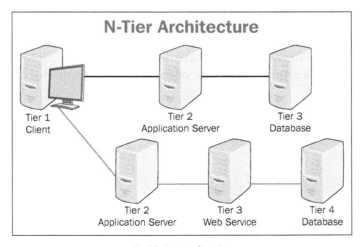

An N-tier application

Now, these tiers which consist of layers will be used to create an enterprise application. But just by making parts of application, we cannot be sure of having a complete solution. Each application has its own challenges, but if we keenly observe them we will find that numerous functionalities are common, irrespective of their problem statement. That means instead of a new team of architect designers fighting for the solution to their problem every time, it will be good to have an answer which is a generic solution for reference. These references will be used to build applications called **design patterns**.

Christopher Alexander says, *Each pattern describes a problem which occurs over and over again in our environment, and then describes the core of the solutions to that problem, in such a way that you can use this solution a million times over without ever doing it the same way twice.*

Each pattern provides a solution to a sort of problem and gives a result quickly. Let's have a quick overview of design patterns. The design patterns are normally classified as creational, structural, and behavioral patterns, which are subclassified as shown in the following table:

Creational design patterns	Structural design patterns	Behavioral design patterns
Singleton pattern	Adapter pattern	Observer pattern
Factory pattern	Composite pattern	Interpreter pattern
Builder pattern	Façade pattern	Chain of responsibility pattern
Prototype pattern	Decorator pattern	Visitor pattern
		Mediator pattern

Frameworks such as Struts and Spring have been built upon these design patterns. Struts uses the front controller design pattern and Spring uses the MVC design pattern for ease of development. The use of frameworks has made the developer's life easy.

Java Enterprise architecture

High performance, faster processing, and good look and feel are the keys to success for enterprise applications. Due to dedicated servers, the tasks of designing, developing, and data storing will be leveraged to handle specialized tasks, as discussed above in the N-tier applications section. In spite of providing just basic things, the N-tier enterprise application needs a bit more. Let's have a look into what else an enterprise application may need.

It's a festive season. The bank has consecutive holidays. I need to withdraw some amount from the ATM, say, for example, x amount. I enter the password and all other required details. Now I am just waiting for the money. I get a message of withdrawal on my mobile as well but... as the ATM doesn't have any money, I haven't received it. The money has been deducted from the account but not received by me. Now what??? Am I going to be in loss? Is there any way to revert what went wrong? Yes, certainly!! Here, we need to take into consideration transaction management. A transaction is a bunch of consecutive operations which take place one after another; either all of these should be completed successfully or none of them. The transaction helps the developer to maintain data integrity. Using this transaction management, the logic has been developed to rollback all such unsuccessful operations. Using this concept, the debited amount can be reversed and credited to my account again. Thank God, I got my money back!!!!

There are many such ATM centers in the city. And the same banking application will be used by many users at the same time. So the application will have multiple requests. All these requests have to be handled in sync. This is possible only if the application supports multithreading, which technically we call **concurrency**.

The ATM is one of the ways to perform banking operations, but today we can even use the Web for these tasks. On the Internet, the request will be sent to the server and further processing happens. As this is a remote process, authentication and authorization is important for recognizing that the user is genuine. This is normally done by using a unique username/password pair which the user enters. The sensitive data will now be transferred through the network; this can be hacked. So such applications should provide secure service layers, which are the URLS with the prefix `https`. We are doing all this to achieve a very important service, that is, security. Security helps to minimize hazardous attacks on the web application.

Do all such services have to be developed by the development team? Well, not completely: in *N* tier applications, we do have a middleware server. This server can also be called a **container**. This container will provide services such as transaction management, security, connection pooling, caching, and concurrency.

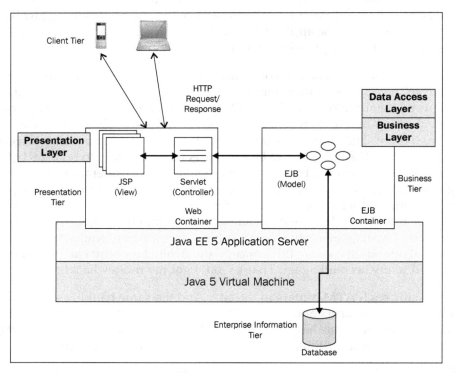

Enterprise architecture

Sharing the work

An enterprise application is always a team effort. It is an application where different teams of designers, developers, and testers work on their respective specialized areas. What is the guarantee that the teams are working from the same facility? No, it's not guaranteed. There is a possibility that they are working from different locations. Now, what is the chance of one team being spread over different locations and they are operating from their locations? This is also quite possible. No, we are not saying that different facilities are our problem. Not really. Our problem is different. Our problem is about the work they have completed. How will others get it? How will they pass on the files created by them or changed by them to other members of their team or to members of other teams? Right, we need to do this manually.

A share folder is a solution only in the case of a local network; for remote, it will not be feasible. If there are a couple of files, we will not face any difficulty but what if there are a number of files? One possible solution can be zipping all the files on which they have worked and mailing it to their teammates. OK, I sent five files. What will other team members do now? They will copy and paste these files in their source code and start using them. We got the solution of exchanging the files. Really??? Do you really think so? As we have seen the scenario only about one member who sent the file and others received, it's true about the reverse case. Others will also send us one or many file similarly. Does each one of us have to copy and paste these files? We are in trouble as we need to share a file to all the team members and we will be getting it from others. So our first problem is how to share files with team members.

Coordinate with the team

Let's discuss one more scenario. Suppose we developed code yesterday and have already shared it with the team. And now our teammates are using it. But now we want to change it because there is a possibility to have one more kind of solution or the client requirement has been changed, or some other reason. A change is never a problem; the problem is in keeping the old code as well as the new one; not only for the one who developed the code, but also the one who received it. Changing the code frequently and keeping it for use frequently is a big problem. It's not only a pain but also frustrating to know what changed, when, and why? We need an easy, practical solution.

The process which helps us to track a file for all of its changes and all of its revisions is called **versioning**. Using versioning, we can keep the original file and all of its step-by-step changes as well. Each changed file will be a new version of the old file. As all of the versions are available, any point when we feel like using a file from xxx version, we just have to get it. We not only store the file but versioning helps to distribute the files so that we will get relief from sharing them manually.

Versioning tools

As versioning has become a very important part of software development, there are many such tools available. These tools are basically divided in two categories:

* Centralized versioning
* Distributed versioning

Centralized versioning

In centralized versioning systems, a copy of the application will be kept on a centralized server from where the developers will take the file or commit their changes to the server. Examples include **Concurrent Versioning System (CVS)** and Subversion.

CVS

CVS is very old tool which was created in the Unix operating system in the 1980s. It was very famous among the developers of Linux and other Unix-based systems; cvslut was developed for Windows servers. CVS uses a central repository of files to record the changes done in any file by the developer in separator directory. If the developer wants his changes be made available to other developers, he will commit the code to the repository. Now, along with the previous version file, the new version also will be recorded.

Though maintaining the main flow of development has made things easy but the branching is not. Sometimes the developers can do parallel development of the products with unique features which they can combine later. This process is called **branching**.

When we rename a file due to some reason or even the location of the file changes, then it is supposed to be tracked by the **SCM (supply chain management)** but CVS cannot update the version in these cases, which is not good.

CVS supports a first come, first served basis, so it's quite possible that some changes will not be reflected or conflicted.

Apache Subversion

Apache Subversion was developed to provide an alternative to CVS. The aim was to fix up the bugs in CVS to maintain high compatibility. It's an open source, where either all the changes will be made or none of them. This feature helps the developers to get the correct, latest revision of the file from the repository. Branching is well supported in SVN.

The best thing about SVN is that a wide range of plugins has been developed, which can be integrated with numerous IDEs to support SVN. The problem of keeping a history of renamed or relocated files has been removed in SVN.

Along with these good things, there are some problems. The biggest problem is what if the SVN server is down? No one will have access and then versioning is not possible. One more issue is about the speed associated with SVN.

Let's now have a discussion in depth about SVN as we are going to use it throughout the book.

As we already know, SVN is an open source version control system which can operate across the network. Its development was started in early 2000 by Collabnet. In initial development, the base was CVS but without the bugs in CVS. This development was started by a team of Karl, Jim, Jason Robbins, and Greg Stein to name a few. This development finished in 2001, from when the developers started using it. Though in the beginning, developers started with CVS as a base, later they started from scratch and developed a fully-fledged new product. In 2009, Collabnet started working with developers to add it to the Apache Software Foundation. They succeeded in 2010.

The architecture of SVN

There are two consistent parts of Subversion: one is the repository which stores all of the versioned data and the other is the client program that manages the local reflections.

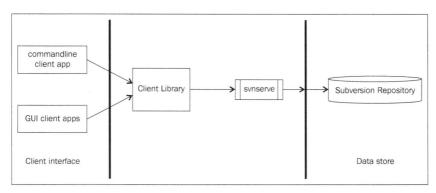

The architecture of Subversion

The repository

The central store where all the versioned data is stored is called the **repository**. The repository normally stores the data in the form of a filesystem tree. A number of clients can get connected with this repository to pass the data in the repository so as to make it available for other teammates. If any teammates want to get the data, they just have to read the repository and the data will be available. The repository keeps a record of each and every version of a file. The repository doesn't only give the reflection of the changes but helps the developer to check what changes have been made, who made them and when. Also, if they are interested in any specific version, they can read it from the repository.

So a version is nothing but a new state of the file where the changes took place.

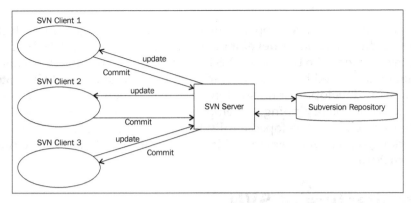

The repository and the sharing of files

Now, we need to understand here the stages of a file.

If any developer creates a new file in his local system, it's not yet known to SVN. So the first task of the developer is to copy this file in SVN, which is called as `svn add`. Whenever we write the file (new or modified) to SVN, the process is called as **committing**. Once the file is committed, it's under SVN and now can be available to other team members. But to use this file, other team members have to take this file into their local system; this will be called as **checkout**. Once any developer gets their file, they are free to use it the way they want. Now, this local copy file will be known as a working copy.

The client program

We can use SVN through the command line. But then we need to remember all the commands for different operations. So instead of using the command line, a UI application can be used. This can be used to commit, checkout, and update the working copy. One such free application with an easy UI is Tortoise SVN, which has been implemented as a Windows shell extension. Using Tortoise SVN, developers can get rid of the command line. Tortoise SVN can easily be integrated in IDEs such as eclipse and Visual Studio.

Distributed versioning

Opposite to centralized versioning, in distributed versioning all the copies of an application will be kept on the developer's machine, for example, GitHub.

GitHub

In opposition with CVS and subversion, GitHub uses a radial approach. The basic idea behind GitHub is to speed up versioning. GitHub is also developed on Linux. But it is also available on Unix native ports of GitHub and Windows operating systems. This being a non-central server, it doesn't lend itself to single developer projects or small projects.

A good thing about GitHub is that it helps the user to navigate through the history of the file. Each instance of the source contains the entire history tree so as to track the changes even when they are not connected to the Internet.

Due to the availability of the tracking of files, branching is well supported by GitHub, but it has limited support for Windows.

Summary

In this chapter, we covered that enterprise applications are the applications which provide solutions to enterprises. These applications consist of huge code. To increase maintainability, performance, and testability, such applications will be developed in tiers. These tiers consist of logical separation of code using layers. Though each layer provides specific functionalities, they have been divided into separate modules. These modules will be developed by a team of developers. To establish coordination, easy sharing and maintaining the history of the files will be done using a versioning tool.

In the next chapter, we will be covering the basics of web applications and developing a sample application using JSP and Servlet. Also, we will be covering the basics of developing a Spring MVC application.

2
Saying Hello to Java EE

To develop a scalable, distributed, well-presented, complex, and multi-layered enterprise application is complicated. The development becomes even worse if the developer is not well aware of the software development fundamentals. Instead of looking at a bigger scenario, if we cut it down into parts and later combine them, it becomes easy for understanding as well as for developing. Each technology has some basics which we cannot overlook. Rather, if we overlook them, it will be the biggest mistake; the same is applicable to Java EE. In this chapter, we are going to explore the following:

- Java EE technologies
- Why servlet and JSP?
- Introduction to Spring MVC
- Creating a sample application through Spring MVC

The enterprise as an application

To withstand the high, competitive, and daily increasing requirements, it's becoming more and more difficult nowadays to develop an enterprise application. The difficulty is due to more than one kind of service, requirement of application to be robust and should support concurrency, security, and many more. Along with these things, enterprise applications should provide an easy user interface but good look and feel for different users. We are going to explore all these things in detail in this as well as in upcoming chapters.

In the last chapter, we discussed enterprise applications. The discussion was more over understanding the terminology or the aspect. Let's now discuss it in terms of development, and what developers look forward to:

- The very first thing even before starting the development is: what we are we developing and why? Yes, as a developer we need to understand the requirements or the expectations from the application. Developers have to develop an application which will meet the requirements.

- The application should be efficient and with high quality so as to sustain in the market.

- The application code should be reliable and bug-free to avoid runtime problems.

- No application is perfect; it's a continuous process to update it for new demands. Develop an application in such a way that it is easy to update.

- To meet high expectations, developers write code which becomes complicated to understand as well as to change. Each one of us wants to have a new and different product, different from what is on the market. To achieve this, designers make an over-clumsy design which is not easy to change in the future. Try to avoid over-complexity both in design and business logic.

- When development starts, developers look forward to providing a solution, but they have to give thought to what they are developing and how the code will be organized in terms of easy maintenance and future extension. Yes, we are thinking about modules which are doing a defined task and those which are less dependent. Try to write a module which will be loosely coupled and highly cohesive.

- Today we are using enterprise applications through different browsers, such as Internet Explorer, Mozilla, or Firefox. We are even using mobile browsers for the same task. This demands an application that has been developed to withstand the number of platforms and browsers.

Going through all this discussion, many technologies come to mind. We will go through one such platform which covers the maximum of the above requirements: the Java Enterprise Edition (Java EE) platform. Let's dive in and explore it!!

The Java EE platform

Sun Microsystems released the Java EE platform in 2000, which was formerly known as the J2EE specification. It defines the standards for developing component-based enterprise applications easily. The concrete implementation is provided by application servers such as Weblogic and GlassFish, and servlet containers such as Tomcat. Today we have Java EE 8 on the market.

Features of the Java EE platform

The following are the various features of the Java EE platform:

- **Platform independency**: Different types of information which the user needs in day-to-day life is spread all over the network on a wide range of platforms. Java EE is well adapted to support, and use this widely spread multiple format information on different platforms easily.

- **Modularity**: The development of enterprise applications is complex and needs to be well organized. The complexity of the application can be reduced by dividing it into different, small modules which perform individual tasks, which allows for easy maintenance and testing. They can be organized in separate layers or tiers. These modules interact with each other to perform a business logic.

- **Reusability**: Enterprise applications need frequent updates to match up client requirements. Inheritance, the fundamental aspect of an object-oriented approach, offers reusability of the components with the help of functions. Java EE offers modularity which can be used individually whenever required.

- **Scalability**: To meet the demands of the growing market, the enterprise application should keep on providing new functionalities to the users. In order to provide these new functionalities, the developers have to change the application. They may add new modules or make changes in already existing ones. Java EE offers well-managed modules which make scalability easy.

The technologies used in Java EE are as follows:

- Java servlet
- Java Server Pages
- Enterprise Java Bean
- Java Messaging API
- XML
- Java Transaction API
- Java Mail
- Web Services

The world of dotcoms

In the 1990s, many people started using computers for a number of reasons. For personal use, it was really good. When it came to enterprise use, it was helpful to speed up the work. But one main drawback was; how to share files, data or information? The computers were in a network but if someone wanted to access the data from any computer then they had to access it personally. Sometimes, they had to learn the programs on that computer, which is not only very time-consuming but also unending.

What if we can use the existing network to share the data remotely?? It was a thought put forward by a British computer scientist, Sir Tim Berners-Lee. He thought of a way to share the data through the network by exploring an emerging technology called **hypertext**. In October 1990, Tim wrote three technologies to fulfill sharing using **Hyper Text Markup Language (HTML)**, **Uniform Resource Identifier (URI)**, and **Hyper Text Transfer Protocol (HTTP)**:

- HTML is a computer language which is used in website creation. Hypertext facilitates clicking on a link to navigate on the Internet. Markups are HTML tags defining what to do with the text they contain.

- URIs defines a resource by location or name of resource, or both. URIs generally refer to a text document or images.

- HTTP is the set of rules for transferring the files on the Web. HTTP runs on the top of TCP/IP.

He also wrote the first web page browser (World Wide Webapp) and the first web server (HTTP). The web server is where the application is hosted. This opened the doors to the new amazing world of the dotcom. This was just the beginning and many more technologies have been added to make the Web more realistic. Using HTTP and HTML, people were able to browse files and get content from remote servers. A little bit of user interaction or dynamicity was only possible through JavaScript. People were using the Web but were not satisfied; they needed something more. Something which was able to generate output in a totally dynamic way, maybe displaying the data which had been obtained from the data store. Something which can manipulate user input and accordingly display the results on the browser.

Java developed one technology: **Common Gateway Interface (CGI)**. As CGI was a small Java program, it was capable of manipulating the data at the server side and producing the result. When any user made a request, the server forward the edit to CGI, which was an external program. We got an output but with two drawbacks:

- Each time the CGI script was called, a new process was created. As we were thinking of a huge number of hits to the server, the CGI became a performance hazard.

- Being an external script, CGI was not capable of taking advantage of server abilities.

To add dynamic content which can overcome the above drawbacks and replace CGI, the servlet was developed by Sun in June 1997.

Servlet – the dynamicity

Servlets are Java programs that generate dynamic output which will be displayed in the browser and hosted on the server. These servers are normally called servlet containers or web servers. These containers are responsible for managing the lifecycle of the servlets and they can take advantage of the capabilities of servers. A single instance of a servlet handles multiple requests through multithreading. This enhances the performance of the application. Let's discuss servlets in depth to understand them better.

The servlet is capable of handling the request (input) from the user and generates the response (output) in HTML dynamically. To create a servlet, we have to write a class which will be extended from GenericServlet or HttpServlet. These classes have service() as a method, to handle request and response. The server manages the lifecycle of a servlet as follows:

1. The servlet will be loaded on arrival of a request by the servers.
2. The instance will be created.
3. The init() will be invoked to do the initialization.
4. The preceding steps will be performed only once in the life cycle of the servlet unless the servlet has not been destroyed.
5. After initialization, the thread will be created separately for each request by the server, and request and response objects will be passed to the servlet thread.
6. The server will call the service() function.
7. The service() function will generate a dynamic page and bind it to the HttpResponse object.
8. Once the response is sent back to the user, the thread will be deallocated.

From the preceding steps, it is pretty clear that the servlet is responsible for:

- Reading the user input
- Manipulating the received input
- Generating the response

A good developer always keeps a rule of thumb in mind that a module should not have more than one responsibility, but here the servlet is doing much more. So this has addressed the first problem in testing the code, maybe we will find a solution for this. But the second issue is about response generation. We cannot neglect a very significant problem in writing well-designed code to have a nice look and feel for the page from the servlet. That means a programmer has to know or adapt designing skills as well, but, why should a servlet be responsible for presentation?

The basic thought of taking presentation out of the servlet leads to **Java Server Page (JSP)**. JSP solves the issue of using highly designed HTML pages. JSP provides the facility of using all HTML tags as well as writing logical code using Java. The designers can create well-designed pages using HTML, where programmers can add code using scriptlet, expression, declaration, or directives. Even standard actions like useBean can be used to take advantage of Java Beans. These JSP's now get transformed, compiled into the servlet by the servers.

Now we have three components:

- Controller, which handles request and response
- Model, which holds data acquired from handling business logic
- View, which does the presentation

Combining these three we have come across a design pattern—**Model-View-Controller (MVC)**. Using MVC design patterns, we are trying to write modules which have a clear separation of work. These modules can be upgradable for future enhancement. These modules can be easily tested as they are less dependent on other modules. The discussion of MVC is incomplete without knowing two architectural flavors of it:

- MVC I architecture
- MVC II architecture

MVC I architecture

In this model, the web application development is page-centric around JSP pages. In MVC I, JSP performs the functionalities of handling a request and response and manipulating the input, as well as producing the output alone. In such web applications, we find a number of JSP pages, each one of them performing different functionalities. MVC I architecture is good for small web applications where less complexity and maintaining the flow is easy. The JSP performs the dual task of business logic and presentation together, which makes it unsuitable for enterprise applications.

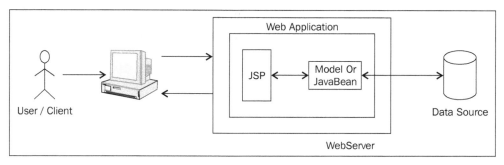

MVC I architecture

MVC II architecture

In MVC II, a more powerful model has been put forward to give a solution to enterprise applications with a clear separation of work. It comprises two components: one is the controller and other the view, as compared to MVC I where view and controller is JSP (view). The servlets are responsible for maintaining the flow (the controller) and JSP to present the data (the view). In MVC II, it's easy for developers to develop business logic- the modules which are reusable. MVC II is more flexible due to responsibility separation.

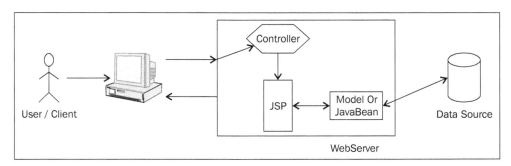

MVC II architecture

The practical aspect

We have traveled a long way. So, instead of moving ahead, let's first develop a web application to accept data from the user and display that using MVC II architecture. We need to perform the following steps:

1. Create a dynamic web application using the name `Ch02_HelloJavaEE`.
2. Find the `servlet-api.jar` file from your `tomcat/lib` folder. Add `servlet-api.jar` to the `lib` folder.

3. Create `index.jsp` containing the form which will accept data from the user.

4. Create a servlet with the name `HelloWorldServlet` in the `com.packt.ch02.servlets` package.

5. Declare the method `doGet(HttpServletRequest req,HttpServletResponse rs)` to perform the following task:

    1. Read the request data using the `HttpServletRequest` object.

    2. Set the MIME type.

    3. Get an object of `PrintWriter`.

    4. Perform the business logic.

    5. Bind the result to the session, application or request scope.

6. Create the view with name `hello.jsp` under the folder `jsps`.

7. Configure the servlet in **deployment descriptor (DD)** for the URL pattern.

8. Use expression language or Java Tag Library to display the model in the JSP page.

Let's develop the code.

The filesystem for the project is shown in the following screenshot:

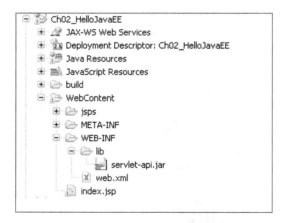

We have created a web application and added the JARs. Let's now add `index.jsp` to accept the data from the user:

```
<form action="HelloWorldServlet">
    <tr>
      <td>NAME:</td>
      <td><input type="text" name="name"></td>
    </tr>
```

```
      <tr>
        <td></td>
        <td><input type="submit" value="ENTER"></td>
      </tr>
  </form>
```

When the user submits the form, the request will be sent to the URL
`HelloWorldServlet`.

Let's create the `HelloWorldServlet` which will get invoked for the above URL,
which will have `doGet()`. Create a model with the name `message`, which we
will display in the view. It is time to forward the request with the help of the
`RequestDispatcher` object. It will be done as follows:

```
protected void doGet(HttpServletRequest request, HttpServletResponse
response) throws ServletException, IOException {
    // TODO Auto-generated method stub
    //read the request parameter
    String name=request.getParameter("name");
    //get the writer
    PrintWriter writer=response.getWriter();

    //set the MIME type
    response.setContentType("text/html");

    // create a model and set it to the scope of request
    request.setAttribute("message","Hello "+name +" From JAVA
Enterprise");
    RequestDispatcher dispatcher=request.getRequestDispatcher("jsps/
hello.jsp");
    dispatcher.forward(request, response);

    }
```

Now create the page `hello.jsp` under the folder `jsps` to display the model `message`
as follows:

```
<h2>${message }</h2>
```

The final step is to configure the servlet which we just have created in DD. The
configuration is made for the URL `HelloWorldServlet` as follows:

```
<servlet>
<servlet-name>HelloWorldServlet</servlet-name>
<servlet-class>com.packt.ch02.servlets.HelloWorldServlet
</servlet-class>
```

```
</servlet>
<servlet-mapping>
<servlet-name>HelloWorldServlet</servlet-name>
<url-pattern>/HelloWorldServlet</url-pattern></servlet-mapping>
```

Let's deploy the application to check the output:

Displaying the home page for a J2EE application

The following screenshot shows the output when a name is entered by the user:

Showing the output when a name is entered by the user

After developing the above application, we now have a sound knowledge of how web development happens, how to manage the flow, and how navigation happens. We can observe one more thing: that whether it's searching data, adding data, or any other kind of operation, there are certain steps which are common, as follows:

- Reading the request data
- Binding this data to a domain object in terms of model data
- Sending the response

We need to perform one or more of the above steps as per the business requirement. Obviously, by only performing the above steps, we will not be able to achieve the end effect but there is no alternative. Let's discuss an example.

We want to manage our contact list. We want to have the facilities for adding a new contact, updating a contact, searching one or many contacts, and deleting a contact. The required data will be taken from the user by asking them to fill in a form. Then the data will be persisted in the database.

Here, for example, we just want to insert the record in the database. We have to start the coding from reading request data, binding it to an object and then our business operation. The programmers have to unnecessarily repeat these steps. Can't they get rid of them? Is it possible to automate this process?? This is the perfect time to discuss frameworks.

What is a framework?

A framework is software which gives generalized solutions to common tasks which occur in application development. It provides a platform which can be used by the developers to build up their application elegantly.

Advantages of frameworks

The advantages of using frameworks are as follows:

- Faster development
- Easy binding of request data to a domain object
- Predefined solutions
- Validations framework

In December 1996, Sun Microsystems published a specification for JavaBean. This specification was about the rules, using which developers can develop reusable, less complex Java components. These POJO classes are now going to be used as a basis for developing a lightweight, less complex, flexible framework: the Spring framework. This framework is from the thoughts of Rod Johnson in February 2003. The Spring framework consists of seven modules:

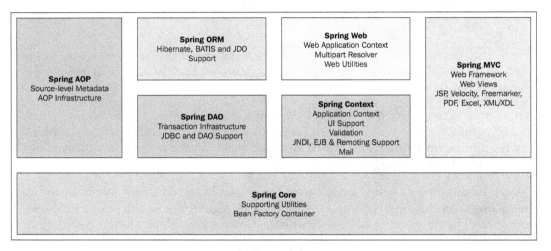

Spring modules

Though Spring consists of several modules, the developer doesn't have to be always dependent on the framework. They can use any module as per the requirement. It's not even compulsory to develop the code which has been dependent upon Spring API. It is called a non-intrusive framework. Spring works on the basis of **dependency injection (DI)**, which makes it easy for integration. Each class which the developer develops has some dependencies. Take the example of JDBC: to obtain a connection, the developer needs to provide URL, username, and password values. Obtaining the connection is dependent on these values so we can call them dependencies, and injection of these dependencies in objects is called DI. This makes the emerging spring framework the top choice for the middle tier or business tier in enterprise applications.

Spring MVC

The spring MVC module is a choice when we look forward for developing web applications. The spring MVC helps to simplify development to develop a robust application. This module can also be used to leave common concerns such as reading request data, data binding to domain object, server-side validation and page rendering to the framework and will concentrate on business logic processes.

That's what, as a developer we were looking for. The spring MVC can be integrated with technologies such as Velocity, Freemarker, Excel, and PDF. They can even take advantage of other services such as aspect-oriented programming for cross-cutting technologies, transaction management, and security provided by the framework.

The components

Let's first try to understand the flow of normal web applications in view of the Spring framework so that it will be easy to discuss the component and all other details:

1. On hitting the URL, the web page will be displayed in the browser.
2. The user will fill in the form and submit it.
3. The front controller intercepts the request.
4. The front controller tries to find the Spring MVC controller and pass the request to it.
5. Business logic will be executed and the generated result is bound to the `ModelAndView`.
6. The `ModelAndView` will be sent back to the front controller.
7. The front controller, with the help of `ViewResolver`, will discover the view, bind the data and send it to the browser.

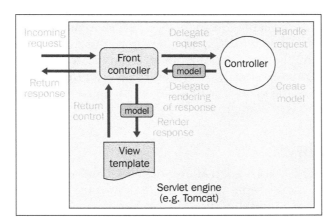

Spring MVC

The front controller

As already seen in servlet JSP to maintain each flow of the application the developer will develop the servlet and data model from servlet will be forwarded to JSP using attributes. There is no single servlet to maintain the application flow completely. This drawback has been overcome in Spring MVC as it depends on the front controller design pattern.

In the front controller design pattern, there will be a single entry point to the application. Whatever URLs are hit by the client, it will be handled by a single piece of the code and then it will delegate the request to the other objects in the application.

In Spring MVC, the `DispatcherServlet` acts as front controller. `DispatcherServlet` takes the decision about which Spring MVC controller the request will be delegated to. In the case of a single Spring MVC controller in the application, the decision is quite easy. But we know in enterprise applications, there are going to be multiple Spring MVC controllers. Here, the front controller needs help to find the correct Spring MVC controller. The helping hand is the configuration file, where the information to discover the Spring MVC controller is configured using handler mapping. Once the Spring MVC controller is found, the front controller will delegate the request to it.

Spring MVC controller

All processes, such as the actual business logic, decision making or manipulation of data, happen in the Spring MVC controller. Once this module completes the operation, it will send the view and the model encapsulated in the object normally in the form of `ModelAndView` to the front controller. The front controller will further resolve the location of the view. The module which helps front controller to obtain the view information is `ViewResolver`.

ModelAndView

The object which holds information about the model and view is called as `ModelAndView`. The model represents the piece of information used by the view for display in the browser of different formats.

ViewResolver

The Spring MVC controller returns `ModelAndView` to the front controller.
The `ViewResolver` interface helps to map the logical view name to the actual
view. In web applications, data can be displayed in a number of formats, from
as simple as JSP to complicated formats like JasperReport. Spring provides
`InternalResourceViewResolver`, `JspViewResolver`, `JasperReportsViewResolver`,
`VelocityLayoutViewResolver`, and so on, to support different view formats.

The configuration file

`DispatcherServlet` needs to discover information about the Spring MVC controller,
`ViewResolver`, and many more. All this information is centrally configured in a file
named `XXX-servlet.xml` where `XXX` is the name of the front controller. Sometimes
the beans will be distributed across multiple configuration files. In this case, extra
configuration has to be made, which we will see later in this chapter.

The basic configuration file will be:

```
<beans xmlns="http://www.springframework.org/schema/beans"
  xmlns:context="http://www.springframework.org/schema/context"
  xmlns:xsi="http://www.w3.org/2001/XMLSchema-instance"
  xsi:schemaLocation="
    http://www.springframework.org/schema/beans
    http://www.springframework.org/schema/beans/spring-beans-3.0.xsd
    http://www.springframework.org/schema/context
http://www.springframework.org/schema/context/spring-context-3.0.xsd">
<!--mapping of the controller -->
<!--bean to be configured here for view resolver  - ->
</beans>
```

The controller configuration file will be named `name_of_servlet-servlet.xml`. In
our project, we will name this `HelloWeb-servlet.xml`.

Let's do the basics of a web application using Spring MVC to accept the data and
display it. We need to perform the following steps:

1. Create a web application named `Ch02_HelloWorld`.
2. Add the required JAR files for Spring (as shown in the following screenshot)
   and servlets in the `lib` folder.
3. Create an index page from where the data can be collected from the user and
   a request sent to the controller.
4. Configure the front controller in DD.

5. Create a SpringMVCcontroller as `HelloWorldController`.

6. Add a method for accepting requests in the controller which performs business logic, and sends the view name and model name along with its value to the front controller.

7. Create an XML file in WEB-INF as `Front_Controller_name-servlet.xml` and configure SpringMVCcontroller and ViewResolver.

8. Create a JSP which acts as a view to display the data with the help of **Expression Language (EL)** and **JavaServer Pages Standard Tag Library (JSTL)**.

Let's create the application.

The filesystem for the project is as follows:

We have already created the dynamic web project `Ch02_HelloSpring` and added the required JAR files in `lib` folder. Let's start by creating `index.jsp` page as:

```
<form action="hello.htm">
    <tr>
      <td>NAME:</td>
      <td><input type="text" name="name"></td>
    </tr>
    <tr>
      <td></td>
      <td><input type="submit" value="ENTER"></td>
    </tr>
</form>
```

When we submit the form, the request is sent to the resource which is mapped for the URL `hello.htm`. Spring MVC follows the front controller design pattern. So all the requests hitting the application will be first attended by the front controller and then it will send it to the respective Spring controllers.

The front controller is mapped in DD as:

```
<servlet>
    <servlet-name>HelloSpring</servlet-name>
    <servlet-class>org.springframework.web.servlet.DispatcherServlet
    </servlet-class>
  </servlet>
  <servlet-mapping>
    <servlet-name>HelloSpring</servlet-name>
    <url-pattern>*.htm</url-pattern>
</servlet-mapping>
```

Now the controller needs help to find the Spring MVC controller. This will be taken care of by the configuration file. This file will have the name `XXX-servlet.xml` where `XXX` is replaced by the name of the front controller from DD. Here, in this case `HelloSpring-servlet.xml` will have the configuration. This file we need to keep in the WEB-INF folder. In the `Configuration` files section, we saw the structure of the file. In this file, the mapping will be done to find out how the package in which the controllers are kept will be configured. This is done as follows:

```
<context:component-scan base-package="com.packt.ch02.controllers" />
```

Now the front controller will find the controller from the package specified as a value of `base-package` attribute. The front controller will now visit `HelloController`. This class has to be annotated by `@Controller`:

```
@Controller
public class HelloController {
//code here
}
```

Once the front controller knows what the controller class is, the task of finding the appropriate method starts. This will be done by matching the values of `@RequestMapping` annotation applied either on the class or on the methods present in the class. In our case, the URL mapping is `hello.htm`. So the method will be developed as:

```
@RequestMapping(value="/hello.htm")
  public ModelAndView sayHello(HttpServletRequest request)
  {
    String name=request.getParameter("name");
```

```
    ModelAndView mv=new ModelAndView();
    mv.setViewName("hello");
    String message="Hello "+name +" From Spring";
    mv.addObject("message",message);
    return mv;
}
```

This method will return a `ModelAndView` object which contains a view name, model name and value for the model. In our code the view name is `hello` and the model is presented by `message`. The Front Controller now again uses `HelloSpring-servlet.xml` for finding the ViewResolver to get the actual name and location of the view. ViewResolver will provide the directory name (location) where the view is placed with a property prefix. The format of the view is given by the property suffix. Using the view name, prefix and suffix, the front controller gets the page. The ViewResolver will bind the model to be used in the view:

```
<bean id="viewResolver"
  class="org.springframework.web.servlet.view.
InternalResourceViewResolver">
    <property name="prefix" value="/WEB-INF/jsps/" />
    <property name="suffix" value=".jsp" />
</bean>
```

In our case, it will be `/WEB-INF/jsps/` as prefix, `hello` as the name of page, and `.jsp` is the suffix value. Combining them, we will get `/WEB-INF/jsps/hello.jsp`, which acts as our view.

The Actual view is written as `prefix+view_name from ModelAndView+suffix`, for instance:

`/WEB-INF/jsps/+hello+.jsp`

The data is bounded by the front controller and the view will be able to use it:

```
<h2>${message}</h2>.
```

Displaying the home page for a Spring application

Entering the name in the text field (for example, **Bob**) and submitting the form gives the following output:

Showing an output when a name is entered by the user

Now we understand the working of spring MVC, let's discuss a few more things required in order to develop the Spring MVC controller.

Each class which we want to discover as the controller should be annotated with the `@Controller` annotation. In this class, there may be number of methods which can be invoked on request. The method which we want to map for URL has to be annotated with the annotation `@RequestMapping`.

There can be more than one method mapped for the same URL but it will be invoked for different HTTP methods. This can be done as follows:

```
@RequestMapping(value="/hello.htm",method= RequestMethod.GET)
  public ModelAndView sayHello(HttpServletRequest request)
  {


  }
@RequestMapping(value="/hello.htm",method= RequestMethod.POST)
  public ModelAndView sayHello(HttpServletRequest request)
  {


  }
```

These methods normally accept Request as parameter and will return `ModelAndView`. But the following return types and parameters are also supported.

The following are some of the supported method argument types:

- `HttpServletRequest`
- `HttpSession`
- `Java.util.Map`/ `org.springframework.ui.Model`/ `org.springframework.ui.ModelMap`
- `@PathVariable`
- `@RequestParam`
- `org.springframework.validation.Errors`/ `org.springframework.validation.BindingResult`

The following are some of the supported method return types:

- `ModelAndView`
- `Model`
- `Map`
- `View`
- `String`
- `void`

Sometimes the bean configuration is scattered in more than one file. For example, we can have controller configuration in one file and database, security-related configuration in a separate file. In that case, we have to add extra configuration in DD to load multiple configuration files, as follows:

```
<servlet>
    <servlet-name>HelloSpring</servlet-name>
    <servlet-class>org.springframework.web.servlet.DispatcherServlet
    </servlet-class>
    <init-param>
        <param-name>contextConfigLocation</param-name>
        <param-value>/WEB-INF/beans.xml</param-value>
    </init-param>
</servlet>
<servlet-mapping>
    <servlet-name>HelloSpring</servlet-name>
    <url-pattern>*.htm</url-pattern>
</servlet-mapping>
```

Summary

In this chapter, we learned how the application will be single-handedly controlled by the front controller, the dispatcher servlet. The actual work of performing business logic and giving the name of the view, data model back will be done by the Spring MVC controller. The view will be resolved by the front controller with the help of the respective ViewResolver. The view will display the data got from the Spring MVC controller. To understand and explore Spring MVC, we need to understand the web layer, business logic layer and data layer in depth using the basics of Spring MVC discussed in this chapter.

We will start with web layers in the next chapter to find out the answers to some questions such as how to handle forms, how to bind form data, and how to do server-side form validation.

3
Implementing the Presentation Layer

In the world of the Web, everything is virtual, where presentation plays the most important role. On the Web, the first thing which can present the product is the presentation, that is, the look and feel. It gives comfort to the user to use the product. A well-presented page attracts more users than an average-looking page. Are we saying that business logic requirements are not so important? Certainly not! We are saying you should make a balance between the good look and feel of the page and the business logic requirements.

In this chapter, we will find out the following:

- How the presentation layer components need to interact with the user
- Spring MVC parameter binding and its implementation
- How to render the presentation layer

Presentation

As said by someone, *The first impression is the best impression*. From the user's perspective, we cannot deny the fact that the product will be more used if it is easy to use and well presented. If the instructions to the user are unclear or complicated, the user tries to avoid using it. If I want to buy a book about J2EE from the bookshop, what will be the first thing which will be visible to me? It is the cover. If the cover is attractive, I will go and at least check out what the content inside is. That will not happen if a book has an average cover and simple presentation. Everyone will obviously check for the quality of the content and the usefulness but that's once we take the book in hand. So to force someone to at least to have a look at it, the most important thing is the presentation!! So we as developers need to make sure that the web page is attractive.

If the page is very well designed with a good color scheme, nice font, use of images as per the theme, clear instruction provided in form navigation, and well-written information, the user will be happy. What about developers? Does the developer need to invest their time because the designers have not paid attention to the form processing? Yes, how the form should be processed is not the designer's concern. But if they had thought about it, the developer's life would be bit easier. What is form processing and why are we fighting for it? Whenever the user submits the form, the information which has been given by the user is important to serve him correctly. Form parameters are the only means to know what the user is interested in. For example, when we want to search for information about Spring MVC, what will we do? Obviously, we will Google it!!! That means:

- We will type the URL: `www.google.com`
- We will enter `Spring MVC` in the text field on Google's web page

How will the web component, in our case the Spring MVC controller, read the string `'Spring MVC'`? The controller will read it from request parameters, which we had filled in the form. To read one or two request parameters is never a problem. But what if a multifield form has to be submitted and then the developer has to read them? Yes, it is not difficult, but you all will agree that it is lengthy work. Each time form submission happens, the same boilerplate code will have to be repeated. Can't we simplify this? Create a web page which will simplify the form-binding process?

In the form, a couple of times there are some fields which have a definite set of values. For example, in a new account opening form (maybe for the bank), the names of branches are available; on a Gmail account, a country list is available; and in online reservations, there are routes or starting and end points well defined. These values are pre-populated because the services are available only in those areas or points and the user should choose from the options available. These pre-populated values can easily be hardcoded by the designer but what if the list or the options are frequently changing? It's better to fetch such values at runtime. **A form should be easily pre-populated**.

Form submission is important, but the form field should have the correct type of values, maybe in terms of the format of the values or the range of values. We normally call this form validation. JavaScript is used as client-side validation. But JavaScript can be turned off. This leads to a serious problem as the form parameter values are the basics of the business logic. The problem can be resolved by doing server-side validation. Hence the page **should support server-side form validation**.

All of the discussed points are well supported by JSPs. Along with HTML in JSP, Java code is well supported. To simplify Java support, a wide range of JSTL, as well as Spring provided tags are available. JSP has support for Expression language where data models can be rendered for runtime values. In Spring, instead of using plain HTML code, we will use Spring provided tags so as to make data binding easier.

Let's have a look at different scenarios to bind the data.

Data binding

Whenever form submission happens, the usual process from the developer side will be to read the request parameters which users have filled in the form. This entered data is in text format. The process of converting this text-based data to the appropriate Java data type is data binding.

When we use the form, it has two criteria:

- Form used for searching data
- Form to retrieve the data and get object values from it

Case 1 – Reading request parameters for searching

Let's create a dynamic web project with Ch03_Search_Form_Data having the following outline. We will use this as the base project to add the further concepts programmatically:

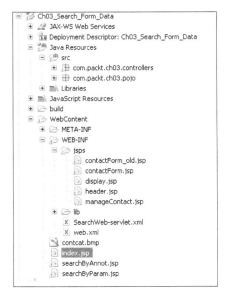

Let's create a form named `SearchByParam.jsp`, which accepts data from the user:

```
<form action="searchFromRequest.htm">
    <tr>
      <td>Enter ID:</td>
      <td><input type="text"name="id"></td>
    </tr>
    <tr>
      <td></td>
      <td><input type="submit"value="Search"></td>
    </tr>
</form>
```

To get this form, we need to add the link `index.jsp` page as follows:

```
<a href="searchByParam.jsp" style="font-size: large;xx-large; font-
family:Times New Roman ; font: bold; width: 300px; height: 200px;
">Search Using Parameter</a><br>
```

The controller code to read the request parameter for search will be:

```
@RequestMapping(value="/searchFromRequest.htm")
  public ModelAndViewsayHello(HttpServletRequest request)
  {
    String name=request.getParameter("id");

    //will add code here to search from persistence layer in Chapter 4
    where we are going to develop the database
    //we will get object and return it to display it in chapter 4

    ModelAndView mv=newModelAndView();
    mv.setViewName("display");
    String message="Hello "+ name;
    mv.addObject("searchObject",message);
    return mv;
  }
```

Instead of reading request parameters one by one from the `HttpServletRequest` object, let's take advantage of Spring and do it all at once as follows:

1. Create a new class `SearchAnnotController` in the `com.packt.ch03.controllers` package.

2. Annotate it with `@Controller` and add the following method to map `/searchFromAnnot.htm`:

```
@RequestMapping(value = "/searchFromAnnot.htm")
  public ModelAndViewsayHello(@RequestParam("id") int id) {
```

```
    //will add code here to search from persistence layer in
Chapter 4 where we are going to develop the database
    //we will get object and return it to display it in chapter 4

    ModelAndView mv = newModelAndView();
    mv.setViewName("display");
    String message = "Hello " + id;
    mv.addObject("searchObject", message);
    return mv;
  }
```

Using @RequestParam, a developer can read a single parameter at a time. Now we don't have to expose servlet APIs.

3. Create a page seachByAnnot.jsp with the following code to accept the data from the user and process it in the method we defined in the preceding step with the code as follows:

```
<body>
<jsp:include page="/WEB-INF/jsps/header.jsp"></jsp:include>
  <center>
    <h1>Please Enter Id to Search</h1>
  </center>
  <table align="center">
    <form action="searchFromAnnot.htm">
      <tr>
        <td>Enter ID:</td>
        <td><input type="text" name="id"></td>
      </tr>

      <tr>
        <td></td>
        <td><input type="submit" value="Search"></td>
      </tr>
    </form>
  </table>
</body>
```

4. To get this form, we need to add the link index.jsp page as follows:

```
<a href="searchByAnnot.jsp" style="font-size: large;xx-large;
font-family:Times New Roman ; font: bold; width: 300px; height:
200px; ">Search Using Annotation</a><br>
```

Case 2 – Reading multiple form fields

We have just seen how to read a single request parameter. Let's now create a form to accept ID, name and address:

```
contactForm_old.jsp
<form method="POST" action="addContact.htm">
    <h2>
      <center>Contact Registration</center>
    </h2>

    <table width="100%" height="150" align="center" border="0">
      <tr>
        <td width="50%" align="right">ID</td>
        <td width="50%" align="left">
<input type="text" name="id" size="30" />
</td>
      </tr>
      <tr>
        <td width="50%" align="right">Name</td>
        <td width="50%" align="left">
<input type="text" name="name" size="30" />
</td>
      </tr>
      <tr>
        <td width="50%" align="right">Address</td>
        <td width="50%" align="left">
<input type="text" name="address" size="30" />
</td>
      </tr>
      <tr>
        <td colspan="2" align="center">
<input type="submit"  value="Add Contact">
</td>
      </tr>

    </table>

  </form>
```

The code in the controller which reads and uses the request parameters will be as follows:

```
@RequestMapping(value = "/searchFromAnnot.htm")
public ModelAndView addContact(@RequestParam("id") int id, @
```

```
RequestParam("name") String name, @RequestParam("address") int
address) {

    //will add code here to search from persistence layer in Chapter 4
where we are going to develop the database
    //we will get object and return it to display it in chapter 4

    ModelAndView mv = newModelAndView();
    mv.setViewName("display");
    String message = "Hello " + id;
      String name= "Name " + name;
      String add = "Address " + address;
    mv.addObject("searchObject", message);
    return mv;
}
```

Though we achieve abstraction, what if there are multiple fields in the form? We need to read them individually using multiple @RequestParam in the method signature.

Let's discuss code to make this simpler using Spring MVC.

We use @RequestParam as we want to get the object of class Contact without reading individual form parameters and then setting them. Here, the reading is done without using servlet APIs but we can still sophisticate the process and get the customized object of Contact. This can be done by using a form backing object followed by reading the data in the controller class.

Form backing object

The object that is used to collect the values which the user has filled in the form is called a **form backing object**. In Spring, the same terminology can be referred to as a **command object**. This object contains the data which the user has filled in and will be able to retrieve in the controller with the help of ModelAttribute. Now the question arises, how to create, get, and use this command object? This can be easily explained with the help of the last example which we just discussed.

The command object collects the values filled by the user. It means that the page where the user fills in the data already needs to have an available object. It won't be possible with HTML tags, but it's quite easy with the tags provided by Spring. When the user submits the form, we will use a command object in the controller. In order to use the command object, we need to change the signature of the addController() method.

Let's start with developing the process of form binding.

1. In order to achieve a `command` object in the form page, we have to add a method which creates the `command` object and makes it available for use. We are going to create an object of class `Contact` available for use.

   Declare the `contact` class (POJO) in `com.packt.03.pojo` with data members `firstName`, `lastName`, `address`, `email` as `String` and `gender` as `int`.

   It will be done as shown in the following code snippet:

```
@RequestMapping("/showForm.htm")
   public ModelAndView showContactForm(HttpServletRequest request,
      HttpServletResponse response, ModelMap map) throws Exception
{

      Contact contact = new Contact();
      map.addAttribute(contact);
      return new ModelAndView("contactForm");
   }
```

   So when the user clicks on a link to get the `contact` form instead of directly navigating to the JSP page to collect data from the user, the page has to be sent by the controller where the command object has been made available for use. In the preceding code, the object of `contact` has been created. This object has been added to `ModelMap` in order to make it available to the form.

2. The form, instead of using HTML tags, will use Spring tags. Using Spring tags, the request parameter values can be automatically set on the `command` object:

   `contactForm.jsp`

```
<form:form modelAttribute="contact" method="POST"
    action="addContact.htm">
    <h2>
      <center>Contact Registration</center>
    </h2>

    <table width="100%" height="150" align="center" border="0">
      <tr>
        <td width="50%" align="right">FIRST NAME</td>
        <td width="50%" align="left"><form:input path="firstName"
size="30" /></td>
      </tr>
      <tr>
        <td width="50%" align="right">LAST NAME</td>
```

```
      <td width="50%" align="left"><form:input path="lastName"
size="30" /></td>
      </tr>
        <tr>
      <td width="50%" align="right">Gender</td>
      <td width="50%" align="left"><form:input path="gender"
size="30" /></td>
      </tr>

      <tr>
        <td width="50%" align="right">Address</td>
        <td width="50%" align="left"><form:input path="address"
            size="30" /></td>
      </tr>

      <tr>
        <td width="50%" align="right">EMAIL</td>
        <td width="50%" align="left"><form:input path="email"
size="30" /></td>
      </tr>

      <tr>
        <td colspan="2" align="center"><input type="submit"
value="Add Contact"></td>
      </tr>

    </table>

  </form:form>
```

To use Spring tags, we have to add the tag directive in the page as follows:

```
<%@ taglib prefix="form"
uri="http://www.springframework.org/tags/form"%>
```

In the preceding code, the form tag contains the very important attribute 'modelAttribute'. This is our command object to which the values entered by the user will be set. When the user submits the form, the method mapped for the URL addContact.htm will be invoked. This method, in order to use the command object, should have one of the parameters as @ModelAttribute. The value of @ModelAttribute will be the value of the attribute "modelAttribute" taken from the form. In our case it is "contact". The code will be as follows:

```
@RequestMapping("/addContact.htm")
  public ModelAndView addContact(@ModelAttribute("contact")Contact
contact) throws Exception {
```

```
    // redirecting to the profile page (profile.jsp)
    ModelAndView modelAndView=new ModelAndView();
    modelAndView.setViewName("manageContact");
    modelAndView.addObject("id",contact.getName());
    return modelAndView;
}
```

We got all the values entered by the user in the object of contact without reading them individually. The Spring framework binds the object and made it available to us. Isn't it great?

Pre-population of forms

We are now aware of form processing. Here, we have to discuss one more specific scenario: **pre-population of forms**. Sometimes, when the form gets displayed in the browser, there are some fields with predefined values. All such values need to be predefined and sent from the server to the browser in order to achieve dynamicity. For example, when we do online reservations, the input field for **To** as well as **From** will display values in a drop-down menu. In the same way, the available stops are also predefined. Let's discuss it here before moving ahead, how to pre-populate a form. The process is quite similar to that of command objects. We need a variable with predefined values available for use in the form. It can be done by adding a method in the Spring MVC controller class, which will create and set the values for the respective object. Such methods need to be annotated by @ModelAttribute. When the Spring MVC controller is invoked, the method which has been annotated by @ModelAttribute will be invoked, which will make the objects available for use.

Let's have a look into a scenario where we are able to implement ModelAttribute. Suppose we want to display the list of genders with values Male and Female in the drop-down menu. We can hardcode these values in the HTML tag. But doing so can create a problem in updating the code every time the values in the drop-down change. We need to have a method which facilitates us to add or remove the values in the list without changing the code. Now let's see how it can be done in the code.

Let's implement pre-population of form in the project. We will create a new project which will be an extension of the previous project Ch03_Search_Form_Data as Ch03_FormHandling:

1. Declare a method which will return a List.

2. Decide the name of the list which can be used in the form to fetch the values and use it at the time of declaration of ModelAttribute.

3. Annotate the method with @ModelAttribute, as shown in the following screenshot:

```
@ModelAttribute("genderList")
  public List<Gender>addGenders() {
    List<Gender> genders = newArrayList<Gender>();
    Gender genderF = newGender();
    genderF.setId(1);
    genderF.setValue("Female");

    Gender genderM = newGender();
    genderM.setId(1);
    genderM.setValue("Male");

    genders.add(genderF);
    genders.add(genderM);
    return genders;
}
```

We need to declare Gender as class in com.packt.ch03.pojo as POJO with ID and value as data members.

Here we have created a list of Genders. This list will be set to a key "genderList", making it available in the form.

Create an updated JSP named contactForm.jsp, where we will use the key "genderList" in **Expression Language** (EL) instead of just gender as the input text field. It can be done as follows:

```
    <tr>
        <tdwidth="50%"align="right">GENDER</td>
        <tdwidth="50%"align="left">
          <form:selectpath="gender">
            <form:optionsitems="${genderList}"
itemValue="id"itemLabel="value" />
          </form:select>
        </td>
    </tr>
For the replacement for,
<tr>
        <td width="50%" align="right">Gender</td>
        <td width="50%" align="left"><form:input path="gender"
          size="30" /></td>
    </tr>
```

The `<form:options>` tag takes three attributes:

- `items:` List from whom to fetch the values
- `itemValue:` The value which will be sent as request parameter
- `itemLabel:` The value which we want to show in the drop-down

The preceding code gives us the following output:

Form pre-processing

As shown in the output, the **Gender** tag has two values: **Female** and **Male**. These values are displayed as a result of iteration through `items`. The **Gender** values to be shown will be fetched from the list using the attribute `'itemLabel'`. The data member id has values 1, 2 respectively. Whenever the user selects any gender, the ID value associated with it will be the value of selection; we did this by the attribute `'itemValue'`.

Let's update `manageContact.jsp` to display the values accepted from the user with the help of EL using `mycontact` as the attribute name declared in the `addContact()`. The updated code snippet will be as follows:

```
<center>
  <jsp:include page="header.jsp"></jsp:include>
  <br>
  <br>
  <br>
  <table border="1">
    <tr>
      <th>First Name</th>
      <th>Last Name</th>
      <th>Gender</th>
      <th>Phone Number</th>
      <th>Email</th>
```

```
          <th>Address</th>
      </tr>
      <tr>
        <th>${mycontact.firstName }</th>
        <th>${mycontact.lastName }</th>
        <th>${mycontact.gender }</th>
        <th>${mycontact.phone_number }</th>
        <th>${mycontact.email }</th>
        <th>${mycontact.address }</th>
      </tr>
    </table>
  </center>
```

We now have an idea about how to develop a flow to read and bind the request parameter. We also know how a form backing object will be used and how to do pre-processing of the form. But when we handle forms, we have to be careful about validating the form. Form validation is important because the developer has developed the logic depending upon the assumption made about the received data. If the data is incorrect, the logic will fail, and so will the application. Generally, form validation is of two types:

- Client-side validation using JavaScript
- Server-side validation

Spring provides a good support for server-side validation. Spring has two different ways to handle server-side validation:

- Validation interface
- Using annotation provided by JSR303

Form validation

Validation is a process which makes sure that the data which the user is entering in the form is of correct format. For example, the user needs to add their mobile number. They can enter their phone number as:

- 9765123456
- 09765123456
- +919765123456

Though we know all of these forms are valid, if the data type is number then the last value, +91 9765123456, will give a number format exception. In the same way, we can face many problems in business logic because of the pre-assumption of the values which the user enters. This may be because of the user's confusion or by mistake. If we don't want to face this problem, we need to clear the user's confusion and provide them with a clear instruction. Even if the instruction is pretty clear, for some reason we cannot deny the fact that the user will enter the incorrect format. To make sure that the Spring MVC controller will get only the correct data, we can do it with the help of Validators.

Spring MVC provides two mechanisms for validations:

- Developing customized validators using Spring validators
- Annotation-based validation

Developing customized validators using Spring validators

To develop custom validators, we need to do the following steps:

1. Write a class which implements the Validator interface.
2. Override the supports() and validate() methods.
3. Update the controller for one of the data members of type Validator using autowiring:

   Autowiring is auto-discovery of the dependencies. The AddController will invoke the validate() method of the validator to perform the validation. The AddController has the validator as a dependency which needs to be injected. We are using @Autowired to inject this dependency automatically.

   In the controller method where we want to trigger the validation, invoke the validator's validate method in order to perform validation.

4. Configure the Validator in the Spring configuration file.
5. Change the JSP page which displays the form such that it will be able to display the validation error messages.

Let's start developing the code.

In developing a custom validator, we need to write a separate class which provides a mechanism for validating the data associated with the object. In order to do this, we need to follow certain steps as follows:

1. Create a dynamic web application `Ch03_FormValidation_interface` which is an extension of `Ch03_FormHandling`. You can either create a replica of it or use the project with the addition of new code which we are going to develop here. The project outline is as shown:

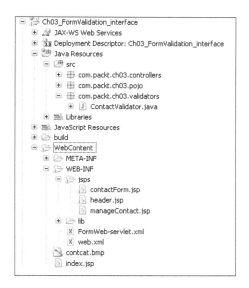

2. Write a class `ContactValidator` which implements the `Validator` interface from the Spring API in the `com.packt.ch03.validators` package:

```
public class ContactValidator implements Validator
{
// implementation goes here
}
```

Override `supports()` to cross-check support type as follows:

```
public boolean supports(Class<?> arg0) {
    // TODO Auto-generated method stub
    return arg0.equals(Contact.class);
  }
```

The `supports()` method checks whether the object to be validated is of the type of the class under validation. Here we are checking for class `Contact`.

3. Override `validate()` methods to write validation logic as follows:

```
public void validate(Object object, Errors errors) {
    // TODO Auto-generated method stub
    Contact contact = (Contact) object;
    if (contact.getFirstName().length() < 2
        || contact.getFirstName().length() > 10) {
      errors.rejectValue("firstName", "name.required",
          "Please Enter First Name");
    }
}
```

The `validate()` method accepts two arguments:

- °   The object whose value we want to validate
- °   If any validation fails, then the information about data binding and validation errors is stored in the `errors` object.

The `rejectValue()` method is used to add a validation error to the `error` object. This method takes three parameters as follows:

- °   The field which the error is associated with
- °   An error code which acts a message key
- °   The message to be shown if validation fails

4. Once the `CustomValidator` is ready, now it's time to use it for validation. In order to use the `Validator`, we need to invoke the `validate()` method in the `AddController`. If any errors are available in validation, we need to show the respective messages in the form in the following steps:

    1. First we need to change the signature of the controller method which gets invoked on form submission to have `BindingResult` in its parameter list.

    2. Invoke the validate method of the `Validator` and pass to it the object to validate and the object of `BindingResult` to whom validation errors will be bounded.

    3. Check whether the object of `BindingResult` has any errors or not. If errors occur, then the same form where the user submits the value has to be returned.

It can be done as shown in the following code snippet:

```
@RequestMapping("/addContact.htm")
  public ModelAndView addContact(@ModelAttribute("contact") Contact
contact,BindingResult result)
      throws Exception {
```

```
    // will add code here to add data to persistence layer
    // we will get object and return it to display it

    validator.validate(contact, result);
    if(result.hasErrors())
    {
      return new ModelAndView("contactForm");
    }

    ModelAndView modelAndView = new ModelAndView();
    modelAndView.setViewName("manageContact");
    modelAndView.addObject("id", contact.getFirstName());
    return modelAndView;
}
```

As we are going to invoke the `validate` method on the `validator`, the controller should have an object available. We will do this by autowiring as follows:

```
@Autowired
Validator validator;
```

Also in the configuration file, we need to configure the bean for the `Validator` class which we have developed. The configuration will look like this:

```
<bean id="validator" class="com.packt.ch03.validators.
ContactValidator"></bean>
```

In case there are validation errors, we need to show them to the user in the same form in front of each field. To do this, the HTML code has to be changed as follows:

```
<tr>
  <td width="50%" align="right">First NAME</td>
  <td width="50%" align="left">
<form:input path="firstName"size="30"/>
    <fontcolor="red">
<form:errors path="firstName"/>
</font>
  </td>
</tr>
```

The tag `<form:errors>` is used to display the validation error message which we have bound in the `validate()` method for the value of attribute 'path'. In this code, we showed how to display a validation error message for the data member `firstName`. In the same way, we can develop the validation for the rest of the fields in the form. After completing the code for validating each and every field in the form, if the user tries to submit it with blank values, the expected output in the browser is as follows:

Form validation using a validator

In the preceding code, we hardcoded the messages to be displayed to the user. We can fetch the values of the messages at runtime using externalization. It can done as follows:

1. Change the code of the validate method as follows:

```java
public void validate(Object object, Errors errors) {
    // TODO Auto-generated method stub
    Contact contact=(Contact)object;
    if(contact.getFirstName().length()<2 || contact.
getFirstName().length()>10)
    {
        errors.rejectValue("firstName","NotEmpty.contact.
firstName");
    }

}
```

   The method `rejectValue()` accepts two parameters: first, the field which the error is associated with and, second, the key whose message value has to be fetched from the properties file.

2. Now we need to specify the messages for the key specified as the second parameter in the `rejectValue()` in the properties file as:

```
NotEmpty.contact.firstName=Please enter your firstname
```

3. Configure the resource bundle in the configuration file so that the Spring container will load it and make it available for use. The configuration will be:

```
<bean id="messageSource" class="org.springframework.context.
support.ReloadableResourceBundleMessageSource">

    <property name="basename" value="/WEB-INF/validations" /></
bean>
```

The property `baseName` defines the location and the name of the properties file where the messages have been configured for the key and its value. We will use this in annotation-based validation in the upcoming application.

Annotation-based validations

To do form validation according to JSR 303 validations, we need to follow these steps:

1. Create a POJO where the data members will be annotated by validation annotations.

2. Write a method in the controller where one of the parameters has a `@Valid` annotation that has values we want to validate and one `BindingResult` argument to bind the validation errors to the field in the form.

3. Write the messages externally in the `properties` file.

4. Configure the properties file in the Spring configuration file.

5. Update JSP using `<form:errors path="XXX"/>` in order to show the validation error messages fetched from the properties file to the user.

Let's start developing the code:

1. Create the dynamic web application `Ch03_FormValidation_Annotation` which is a replica of `Ch03_FormHandling`.

2. Update the POJO class `Contact` where we apply the annotations on the data members. It will be done as follows:

```
public class Contact {
  @NotEmpty
  @Length(min=2,max=10)
  private String firstName;
  @NotEmpty
  private String lastName;

  private int gender;
  @NotEmpty
  private String address;
```

```
@NotEmpty
@Email
private String email;

@NotEmpty
@Pattern(regexp="(^$|[0-9]{10})")
private String phone_number;
// getter and setter method
}
```

All the data members to whom validation is applicable will be annotated with respective annotation. Here we have applied annotation to check whether a particular value is empty, has a particular length, and is a valid e-mail and phone number.

3. This validation has to be triggered in order to perform validations. One of the ways to do the triggering is applying @Valid annotation on the parameter of the type which is under our validation criteria. The code of the controller method which accepts the data from the submitted form will look like:

```
@RequestMapping("/addContact.htm")
  public ModelAndView addContact(
      @Valid@ModelAttribute("contact") Contact contact,
      BindingResult result) throws Exception {
    if (result.hasErrors()) {
      return new ModelAndView("contactForm");
    }
      return new ModelAndView("manageContact", "id", contact.
getEmail());
    }
```

We already discussed the use of @ModelAttribute in order to accept the object. As we are interested in validating the same object, we have to apply @Valid before this parameter, as shown in the code. In order to bind the validation error messages which will be shown to the user, we need BindingResult.

4. Now we need to configure the filename where we are going to put all the error messages. It will be done by configuring the bean messageSource, which will tell the framework the base name of the message file, as follows:

```
<bean id="messageSource"
    class="org.springframework.context.support.
ReloadableResourceBundleMessageSource">
    <property name="basename"value="/WEB-INF/validations"/>
  </bean>
```

5. Update JSP using the following code in order to show the validation error messages fetched from the properties file to the user:

```
<form:errors path="XXX"/>
```

Here, xxx is the property of the POJO class whose object is expected on the form submission.

Let's start developing the `properties` file for showing the messages to the users whenever some validation fails:

1. Create a `validations.properties` file under `WEB-INF` to configure the messages. It will be done as follows:

```
NotEmpty.contact.firstName=Pleaseenteryourfirstname.
NotEmpty.contact.lastName=Pleaseenteryourlastname.

NotEmpty.contact.address=Pleaseenteryouraddress.

NotEmpty.contact.phone_number=Pleaseenteryourphonenumber.
Pattern.contact.phone_number=pleaseentervalid10digitphonenumber

NotEmpty.contact.email=Pleaseenteryoure-mail.
Email.contact.email=Youre-mailisincorrect.
```

2. We need to configure the location and the base name of the properties file in the Spring configuration file so that Spring will load these messages at runtime before the page is rendered in the browser. The configuration will be as follows:

```
<bean id="messageSource"
  class="org.springframework.context.support.
ReloadableResourceBundleMessageSource">
    <property name="basename"value="/WEB-INF/validations"/>
  </bean>
```

The property base name has the value `/WEB-INF/validations`, where `/WEB-INF` is the location where the `properties` file will be available and it will have the base name `validations`.

3. The final step is to show the validation error messages to the user. It can be done using the `<form:errors>` tag as follows:

```
<tr>
      <tdwidth="50%"align="right">FIRST NAME</td>
      <tdwidth="50%"align="left">
<form:input path="firstName"size="30" />
        <fontcolor="red">
```

```
<form:errors path="firstName" />
</font>
        </td>
    </tr>
```

Here we have designed it so that if validation fails for the data member `firstName`, the message will be shown in red color.

The final output on submitting the form with some validation errors will be as follows:

Form validation using annotation

Let's dig into annotation validations bit more.

Spring supports JSR-303. JSR-303 is a specification for bean validation. It's developed for providing a generalized validation solution which the developers need for the model constraints. The developers can reduce the code by using the `HibernateValidator` framework along with Spring. The following are the few validations which the developer uses frequently to put constraints on the fields or properties:

Annotation	Use
`@Length(min=, max=)`	Validate that the annotated string is between `min` and `max`included
`@Max`	Check whether the annotated value is less than or equal to the specified maximum
`@Min`	Check whether the annotated value is higher than or equal to the specified minimum
`@NotNull`	Check that the annotated value is not null
`@NotEmpty`	Check whether the annotated element is not null nor empty
`@NotBlank`	Check that the annotated string is not null and the trimmed length is greater than 0

Annotation	Use
`@Pattern(regex=, flag=`	Check if the annotated string matches the regular expression regex considering the given `flag`match
`@Size(min=, max=)`	Check if the annotated element size is between `min` and `max` (inclusive)
`@Valid`	Perform validation recursively on the associated object

Instead of hardcoding the values, it's always best to externalize them in `properties` files. The name and location can be anything. We just need to take care of configuring whatever the name of the file and the location of file is that we selected in the Spring configuration file. This `properties` file will contain the data in the format of:

```
Key = value
```

The format which we followed while writing the `properties` file to externalize the messages is:

```
Annotation_name.attribute_name.property_name = message to show
```

In our case we used:

```
NotEmpty.contact.firstName=Pleaseenteryourfirstname
```

Now we have an idea about handling a form, it's time to handle the data. The data which we just want to show to the user, we want the user to select the record to be deleted from the drop-down menu are the situations where the data is expected to be retrieved from Spring controller. In order to make the data available for use in the presentation page, we have to add it to the `ModelMap` object. This object can then be used to fetch the values associated with it.

Let's take the example of displaying a contact list in a browser. As we have not yet created a database and related persistence layer we will use static data here. Follow the steps to add the functionality of displaying the data:

1. Add a link **Show All Records** to the index page with **showRecords.htm** as an action URL.

2. Add the `showAllContacts(ModelMap map)` method in the `AddController` class, having URL mapping '**showRecords.htm**'.

3. Implement the method to create a list of contacts and add it to the `map` object and return the view where the contact list can be displayed.

4. Create `showContact.jsp`. Use JSTL's out and `forEach` tag for displaying the data.

Now we know what the steps are, let us start the implementation:

1. Add the following code to add a link:

    ```
    <a href="showRecords.htm">Show All Records</a> in index.jsp.
    ```

2. When the user clicks the link, a method mapped for `showRecord.htm` as a URL pattern will get invoked. In our case, we created `showAllContact()` annotated with `@RequestMapping`. This method will have the code to create a list of contacts by creating some objects of the `Contact` class and then adding them to the array list. Finally, add the list to the object of `ModelMap` as an attribute. We declared the attribute name as `'myList'`. Now return the view `'showContacts'` if the list is not empty. If the list is empty, then return `'error'`. The method will look like this:

    ```
    @RequestMapping("/showRecords.htm")
     public ModelAndView showAllContacts(ModelMap map)
     {
        List< Contact> contacts=new ArrayList<Contact>();

        Contact contact=new Contact();
        contact.setAddress("Pune");
        contact.setEmail("John@gmail.com");
        contact.setFirstName("John");
        contact.setLastName("Ray");
        contact.setGender(0);
        contact.setPhone_number("9856434562");
        Contact contact1=new Contact();
        contact1.setAddress("Mumbai");
        contact1.setEmail("Sonia@gmail.com");
        contact1.setFirstName("Sonai");
        contact1.setLastName("Rai");
        contact1.setGender(1);
        contact1.setPhone_number("9566434160");

        contacts.add(contact);
        contacts.add(contact1);

        if(contacts.size()>0)
        {
          map.addAttribute("myList",contacts);
          return new ModelAndView("showContacts");
        }
        return new ModelAndView("error");
     }
    ```

3. Create the `showContacts.jsp` page which will have the declaration of the JSTL tag library as:

    ```
    <%@taglib prefix="c" uri="http://java.sun.com/jsp/jstl/core"%>
    ```

As we want to display the list, the best choice is a `forEach` tag from JSTL. It can be done as follows:

```
<c:forEach var="record"items="${myList}"varStatus="st">
    <tr>
      <td><c:outvalue="${ record.firstName }"></c:out></td>
      <td><c:outvalue="${ record.lastName }"></c:out></td>
      <td><c:outvalue="${ record.email }"></c:out></td>
      <td><c:outvalue="${ record.phone_number }"></c:out></td>
    </tr>
</c:forEach>
```

The attribute which has be added as an attribute to the object of `ModelMap` is `myList`. We can use it as the value for the attribute `items` using EL. On each iteration, one contact record will be returned, which is going to be stored in the attribute `var`. This value attribute will fetch the value of an individual property using EL as `${ record.firstName}`, where record is the value of the `var` attribute. This attribute temporarily holds the value of one object while iterating through the list. `firstName` is the property name of the object whose data we had stored in the list. We will get the output as follows:

Contact List

First Name	Last Name	Email	Phone Number
John	Ray	John@gmail.com	9856434562
Sonai	Rai	Sonia@gmail.com	9566434160

Data processing using JSTL

Summary

In this chapter, we learned about the presentation layer. We saw how to handle the data taken from the user, how to process form submission, and how to do pre-processing of the form. We also saw server-side form validations and covered the process of displaying the data back to the user. In this chapter, we collected the data from the user but we did not see how to add the data to the persistence layer or how to take data from the persistence layer and then display it to the user.

In the next chapter, we will discuss the persistence layer, using the information about form handling which we just discussed. So let's move on to the exciting world of data persistency!

4
Talking to the Database

On the web, browsing is a common task. The data for which the user is searching will be defined and stored somewhere so that it can be used whenever required. It is not necessarily only in a database; it can be in any format. Can we imagine a dynamic Web without storing data?? Quite difficult to imagine!! Starting from the login to the application and searching for a particular product from the user's perspective, adding new products or updating the existing products from an administrative perspective, in every stage we handle data. In the previous chapter, where we discussed the presentation layer, we were accepting data from the user for registration, searching for a particular ID or when we needed to show the data to the user. But we were not able to save the data as there was no persistency layer included by us.

In this chapter, we will add the persistence layer and find out the following:

- How to implement the persistence layer to take data from the user
- How to communicate with the persistence layer using Spring's Hibernate template
- How to set up JUnit and how to use it for testing a unit

Persistence

Data storage is a very common and basic requirement of enterprise applications. Data storage ensures that the data collected from the user will be saved over time. The mechanism of saving data for the duration so as to make it available later is called **persistency**.

In Java, normally the persistency is of an object. Java can save an object state using the following ways:

- Object serialization
- Storing data in XML format
- Saving the data in a relational database

Using object serialization

The process by which an object is saved across the network is **serialization**. In Java, an object is saved in the file. So we can even say, saving an object to the file is serialization.

Disadvantages of using object serialization

The disadvantages of object serialization are as follows:

- Serialization adds resource overhead
- Serialization is slow

Storing data in XML

In the past few years, XML has emerged as a favorite choice to handle data in a file using markups. The good thing is, the developer can use their own tags to represent the data collection.

Disadvantages of storing data in XML

The disadvantages of storing data in XML are as follows:

- XML needs adequate processing applications
- XML is not for displaying in a browser but for holding data. Not all browsers have inbuilt support. Developers need to use **XSLT** (**extensible stylesheet language**) to present the data on browsers

Saving the data in a relational database

An object consists of data members to present its state. The relational database consists of a table structure which has a row and column structure. One row in a table is mapped to one object. Mapping is a technique that places an object's data members in one or more fields of a database table. The relational database uses an easy query writing mechanism to deal with the stored data. Over the years, the relational database has become the choice of Java developers for achieving persistency.

Advantages of saving data in a relational database

The advantages of saving data in a relational database are as follows:

- It supports easy mapping of a table in the database to object data members
- It has techniques such as primary key, timestamps and version numbers to update an object as and when required
- It provides mapping techniques that can support Java inheritance
- It supports relational mappings such as one to one, one to many, and many to many, which can be used to map Java collections and arrays

Interaction of Java with relational databases

Java is a pure **object-oriented programming** (**OOP**) language while relational databases use **sequential programming language** (**SQL**). Both of them have their own data type, methods and programming techniques. OOP manages objects where SQL manages tables. It is pretty clear that both of them cannot communicate directly with each other due to the unavailability of compatible language support. Direct communication is not possible so the unit is required to make them communicate even though these two are fundamentally different. The **Java Database Connectivity** (**JDBC**) architecture will be managed by JDBC APIs from a Java application which helps to manage the incompetency. The one which manages the language and data type difference is `DriverManager`. The following figure illustrates this:

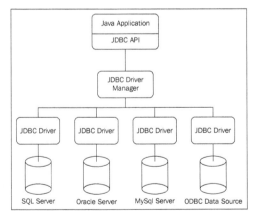

JDBC architecture

The JDBC driver is an implementation that defines the interface in JDBC API for interacting with the database server.

Types of JDBC drivers

The four types of drivers that facilitate JDBC programming on the variety of platforms and operating systems are as follows:

- JDBC-ODBC bridge driver
- JDBC Native API Driver / Partly JAVA Driver
- JDBC Net Protocol Driver
- All Java drivers

We shall now see all types of driver and their advantages and disadvantages.

JDBC-ODBC bridge driver

The Type 1 driver uses JDBC API to the **Open Database Connectivity (ODBC)** API to access a database. The Type 1 driver is installed on the client machine which translates all the JDBC calls into ODBC calls. In order to connect to the database it uses an ODBC driver with the help of **Data Source Name (DSN)**.

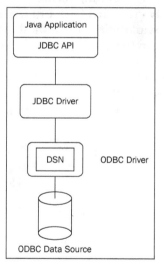

JDBC-ODBC bridge driver

Advantages of the JDBC-ODBC bridge driver

These types of drivers are freely installed on the system, which allows access to almost all types of databases.

Disadvantages of the JDBC-ODBC bridge driver

The disadvantages of using the JDBC-ODBC bridge driver are as follows:

- When a program executes the JDBC, the call gets converted first of all to JDBC-ODBC and then later from JDBC-ODBC to ODBC. As there are a high number of conversions, the working of the driver is slow, which hampers performance.

- The JDBC-ODBC Driver uses system installations so in order to use a Type 1 driver, the ODBC driver needs to be installed on the client system.

- The Type 1 driver uses DSN, which needs to be created on every client machine to connect with a database. This leads to restricting the use of the application to desktops. It's not useful for web applications.

JDBC Native API Driver/Partly Java Driver

The Type 2 Driver converts JDBC calls to the native calls of the database API, which are database specific. It needs some binary code to be present on the client machine to have communication with the database server.

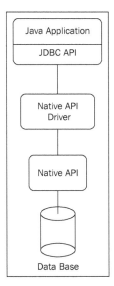

JDBC Native API Driver/Partly JAVA Driver

Advantages of the JDBC Native API Driver

The advantage of using the JDBC Native API Driver is as follows:

- In comparison with the Type 1 driver, it gives better performance

Disadvantages of the JDBC Native API Driver

The disadvantages of using the JDBC Native API Driver are as follows:

- As a vendor-specific native API must be installed on each client machine, it leads to problems using it for the Internet
- The communication with the database server is dependent upon the native API, which leads to problems when the database changes

JDBC Net Protocol Driver

The Type 3 is useful in the case of a middleware server. The JDBC application will send the request to this middleware server, which translates JDBC calls to the respective database.

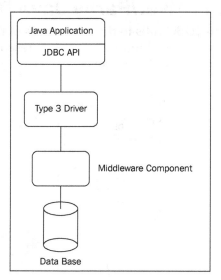

JDBC Net Protocol Driver

Advantages of the JDBC Net Protocol Driver

The advantages of using the JDBC Net Protocol Driver are as follows:

- Unlike the Type 2 driver, in the Type 3 driver there is no need for a vendor-specific database library to be present on each and every machine
- It is portable as it is written in Java
- It can be used for web applications as there is no client-specific code or configuration

Disadvantages of the JDBC Net Protocol Driver

As the Type 3 driver uses a middleware server, it's required to install a separate server application where database-specific coding needs to be performed.

All Java drivers

The Type 4 drivers are also called pure Java drivers as they are completely written in Java. The Type 4 driver converts JDBC calls directly to the database-specific protocol with minimum conversions.

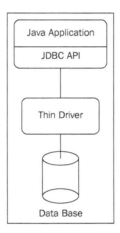

Pure Java driver

Advantage of Java drivers

The advantage of Java drivers is as follows:

- The conversion of calls is from JDBC API to database-specific calls, leading to the best performance among all other drivers

Disadvantages of the Java Driver

The disadvantage of the Java Drivers is as follows:

- As Type 4 driver is specific to the database, whenever the database changes the driver has to be changed accordingly

Let's look at a JDBC application which will insert contact details in the MySQL database using Type 4 driver with the help of the following steps:

1. Register Type 4 driver of MYSQL.
2. Get a `Connection` object.
3. Fire the query using `PreparedStatement` to insert a record.
4. Close all resources.
5. Add the required JAR files for MySQL.

Let's start the development:

1. Create a new Java application `Ch04_ContactManagement`.
2. Create or copy the `Contact` and `Gender` POJOs which we used in previous examples.
3. Create a new interface as `ContactDAO` in `com.packt.ch04.dao` package as follows:

```
public interface ContactDAO {
int addContact(Contact contact);
}
```

4. DAO is a Data Access Object which provides an interface to the database or persistence mechanism. It provides data operations without exposing the actual implementations. The examples which we are going to take while explaining how to handle databases will practically show the power of DAOs.
5. Create a class `ContactDAOImpl` in package `com.packt.ch04.dao` which implements `ContactDAO`.
6. Add a data member `Connection` in `ContactDAOImpl` and initialize it in a constructor. As we are using Type 4 driver for MySQL, the code will be as follows for registering the driver:

```
Class.forName("com.mysql.jdbc.Driver");
```

 Handle the `ClassNotFoundException`.

7. To obtain a `Connection` object, we need to pass the URL, username and password as:

```
connection=DriverManager.getConnection("jdbc:mysql:3306/localhost/
contactDB","root","mysql");
```

8. Implement the method `addContactdecalred` in the `ContactDAO` interface. In this we will fire the query to insert a record in the `Contact_CORE` table with runtime values. The code snippet will be as follows:

```
public int addContact(Contact contact)
  {
    int record=0;
    try {
      PreparedStatement ps=connection.prepareStatement("insert
into Contact_CORE values(?,?,?,?,?,?)");
      ps.setString(1,contact.getFirstName());
      ps.setString(2,contact.getLastName());
      ps.setInt(3,contact.getGender());
      ps.setString(4,contact.getAddress());
      ps.setString(5,contact.getEmail());
      ps.setString(6,contact.getPhone_number());
      record=ps.executeUpdate();
    } catch (SQLException e) {
      // TODO Auto-generated catch block
      e.printStackTrace();
    }
    return record;
  }
```

9. Let's now create `ContactMain` with a `main` function as follows:

```
public static void main(String[] args) {
    // TODO Auto-generated method stub
    ContactDAO contactDAO=new ContactDAOImpl();
    Contact contact=new Contact();
    contact.setFirstName("John");
    contact.setLastName("Ray");
    contact.setGender(1);
    contact.setAddress("JB Road");
    contact.setEmail("john@gmail.com");
    contact.setPhone_number("9845321234");
    int record=contactDAO.addContact(contact);
    if(record==1)
    {
      System.out.println("RECORD INSERTED SUCCESSFULLY");
    }
    else {
      System.out.println("RECORD NOT INSERTED PLEASE TRY AGAIN");
    }
  }
```

Here we are adding hardcoded values just for checking but we can even write code to take data from the user.

10. Now add the `mysql-connector` JAR file. You can download it from `http://www.java2s.com/Code/Jar/m/Downloadmysqlconnectorjar.htm` or `https://dev.mysql.com/downloads/connector/j/3.1.html`.

11. Finally, set up the MySQL database by creating the database and `contact_core` table. We can set up the database as follows:

```
Create database contactDB.

Use contactDB.

Create table Contact_core(firstname varchar(20),lastname
varchar(20),gender int,address varchar(100),email
varchar(20),phone_number varchar(20)).
```

12. The same schema will be used throughout this book.

13. Execute the main code; if there is no exception, one row will be added to the MySQL database. We can check it on the MySQL console as follows:

```
mysql> select * from contact_core;
+-----------+----------+--------+---------+----------------+--------------+
| firstname | lastname | gender | address | email          | phone_number |
+-----------+----------+--------+---------+----------------+--------------+
| John      | Ray      |      1 | JB Road | john@gmail.com | 9845321234   |
+-----------+----------+--------+---------+----------------+--------------+
1 row in set (0.00 sec)
```

MYSQL output

Now we know the basics of databases, let's find out how to do Spring-JDBC integration.

Spring-JDBC integration

In the previous code, we managed the connection, wrote the JDBC query and then obtained the results. Spring gives us the facility to manage these things by the framework. We will move ahead step by step in order to understand the integration completely.

In databases, in every task the developer always needs to obtain the database connection. Spring acquires this connection through the Spring `DataSource`. The `DataSource` is part of the Spring JDBC specification. This means that the developer is not involved in the details of how to obtain the `Connection`. The complete responsibility of getting and maintaining objects will be taken care of by the Spring framework.

Configuring DataSource in Spring JDBC

Spring offers three different ways to configure a DataSource bean:

- Getting data sources by looking up using JNDI
- Getting data sources from the JDBC driver
- Getting data sources that pool connections have configured on a server

Let's see each configuration one by one.

Getting data sources by looking up using JNDI

The Spring MVC application gets deployed on the application as well as web servers. Both types of server allow developers to configure DataSource, which facilitates using container implementations. The **Java Naming and Directory Interface (JNDI)** is an API for directory service which allows Java applications to find objects by name using a lookup mechanism. As the JNDI will be managed by the servers and will be used by the developers through a lookup mechanism, it provides great performance.

The JNDI can be configured as follows:

```
<jee:jndi-lookup id="dataSource"jndi-name="/jdbc/contactDS"
resource-ref="true" />
```

Here:

- jndi-name is name of resource in JNDI
- resource-ref is the value given in jndi-name, which can be prefixed with java:comp/env/

Getting data sources that pool connections configured on a server

Spring does not provide any pooled data source directly. But it provides support for integrating **Jakarta Commons Database Connection Pooling (DBCP)**. The configuration of the BasicDataSourec bean will be:

```
<bean id="dataSource"
class="org.apache.commons.dbcp.BasicDataSource">
<property name="driverClassName" value="com.mysql.jdbc.Driver" />
<property name="url"
value=" jdbc:mysql://localhost:3306/TEST" />
<property name="username" value="root" />
<property name="password" value="mysql" />
```

```
<property name="initialSize" value="5" />
<property name="maxActive" value="10" />
</bean>
```

Getting data sources from the JDBC driver

This is the simplest way to configure the JDBC driver. There are two classes offered by Spring which can be used to get reference of data sources, as follows:

- **DriverManagerDataSource**: The `DriverManagerDataSource` class returns a new connection every time that the developer requests for the connection along with multithreading support.

- **SingleConnectionDataSource**: The `SingleConnectionDataSource` returns the same connection every time a connection is requested by the developer. As every time the same object is returned, it doesn't perform well in multithreaded applications.

The way in which we are going to configure the data source is as follows:

```
<bean id="dataSource"
class="org.springframework.jdbc.datasource.DriverManagerDataSource">
    <property name="driverClassName" value="com.mysql.jdbc.Driver" />
    <property name="url" value="jdbc:mysql://localhost:3306/TEST" />
    <property name="username" value="root" />
    <property name="password" value="mysql" />
</bean>
```

Both of these cannot provide support for a connection pool.

Types of integration of JDBC

We can use the integration of JDBC in the following three ways:

- Integrating the `DataSource` to get a connection reference
- Integrating `JDBCTemplate`
- Integrating `JdbcDaoSupport`

They are explained in the following sections.

Integrating the DataSource to get a connection reference

This is similar to using JDBC API, where the developer is responsible for managing everything related to the database. The following are the steps which can be used in order to leverage Spring to manage the connection:

1. Create a DAO class which has `DataSource` as a data member.
2. Use this `DataSource` to get the connection object.
3. Use the connection object to get `Statement`, `PreparedStatement` to execute the query.
4. Configure the `DataSource` and the DAO class whose data member is `DataSource` in XML file.

Let's start redeveloping the application `Ch03_FormValidation_Annotation`, which we developed in the previous chapter for managing contacts. We will add a database layer in order to maintain persistence. We will add extra code to achieve this by the following steps:

1. Create a new interface `ContactDAO` in the package `com.packt.ch04.dao`. Declare `addContact()` method as:

   ```
   public int addContact(Contact contact);
   ```

2. Implement this interface by `ContactDAOImpl`.
3. In `ContactDAOImpl`, declare a data member of type `DataSource` as follows:

   ```
   private DataSource dataSource;
   ```

4. Create getter and setters for the `DataSource`.
5. Create `addContact(Contact contact)` where we will use the `DataSource` reference to create the `Connection` object. Using the `Connection` object, we will insert the data in the database. The code snippet will be:

   ```
   public int addContact(Contact contact) {
       // TODO Auto-generated method stub
       int record = 0;
       try {
         Connection connection = dataSource.getConnection();
         PreparedStatement ps = connection
             .prepareStatement("insert into Contact_CORE
   values(?,?,?,?,?,?)");
         ps.setString(1, contact.getFirstName());
         ps.setString(2, contact.getLastName());
         ps.setInt(3, contact.getGender());
   ```

```
        ps.setString(4, contact.getAddress());
        ps.setString(5, contact.getEmail());
        ps.setString(6, contact.getPhone_number());
        record = ps.executeUpdate();

    } catch (SQLException e) {
        // TODO Auto-generated catch block
        e.printStackTrace();
    }

    return record;
}
```

6. We have used `dataSource` but we haven't initialized it. We will configure the `dataSource` in the XML file so that the Spring container will initialize it and then with the help of DI we will inject it in the `ContactDAOImpl`. Let's now configure the `dataSource` and `ContactDAOImpl` in `connection.xml` as follows:

```xml
<bean id="dataSource"
class="org.springframework.jdbc.datasource.
DriverManagerDataSource">
    <property name="driverClassName" value="com.mysql.jdbc.Driver" />
    <property name="url" value="jdbc:mysql://localhost:3306/
contactDB" />
    <property name="username" value="root" />
    <property name="password" value="mysql" />
</bean>

<bean id="contactDao" class="com.packt.ch04.dao.ContactDAOImpl">
    <property name="dataSource" ref="dataSource" />
</bean>
```

 The values used in the preceding code for `driverClassName`, `url`, `username` and `password` will be the values which enable us to connect to the database for the respective Type 4 driver for the MySQL database.

7. The database layer will be used by the controller so the controller should have reference to the `ContactDAO`. It can be done by adding the code in class `AddController` as follows:

```
@Autowired
ContactDAO contactDAO;
```

8. Update the `addContact()` method in the controller to invoke `addContact()` from the DAO class. The code snippet will be:

```
@RequestMapping("/addContact.htm")
  public ModelAndView addContact(
      @Valid@ModelAttribute("contact") Contact contact,
      BindingResult result) throws Exception {
    if (result.hasErrors()) {
    return new ModelAndView("contactForm");
    } else {
    int record = contactDAO.addContact(contact);
    if (record > 0) {
      return new ModelAndView("manageContact", "id",
          contact.getEmail());
    }
    }
    return new ModelAndView("contactForm","error","Data Cannot be
inserted Email is already registered");
  }
```

9. After deploying the code, the output where the user will fill up the data for a new contact will be as follows:

Contact Registration

FIRST NAME	Anudnya
LAST NAME	Prabhakaran
GENDER	F
ADDRESS	Hydrabad
PHONE NUMBER	7687654781
EMAIL	anudnya@abc.com

Add Contact

Contact registration form

10. When the user clicks on **Add Contact**, if the e-mail ID is not already in the database, we will get a success message as follows:

Managing contacts
ID:- anudnya@abc.com

Contact registration form

Here, ID is the e-mail the user entered in the contact registration form. We can check the data in the table `Contact_CORE` under the `contactDB` schema.

Integrating the JDBC template

In JDBC, the burden of managing the database, firing the queries and handling the exceptions is always on the development side. Spring helps to clean the code and facilitates the developer to write only necessary code. The template provides the facility to the developer to develop a DAO version specific to their application problem. The injection of the template is good for abstraction. Spring provides three template classes to be chosen by the developer:

- **JdbcTemplate**: The `PreparedStatement` facilitates firing a query to the database using runtime values by specifying the index of the parameter. `JdbcTemplate` also facilitates querying the database using a similar kind of indexing.

- **NamedParameterJdbcTemplate**: The `NamedParameterJdbcTemplate` class enables the developer to query the database with binding the parameters with the help of a name in a SQL query rather than indexing as done in `JdbcTemplate`.

- **SimpleJdbcTemplate**: This class is similar to `JdbcTemplate` with one major advantage of supporting Java 5 features.

Let's redevelop the application which we developed in case 1 using `JDBCTemplate` instead of using `DataSource` using the following steps:

1. Let's change the implementation of `ContactDAOImpl` by declaring a data member of type `JdbcTemplate` instead of `DataSource` as:

   ```
   JdbcTemplate jdbcTemplate;
   ```

2. Add getter and setters for `JdbcTemplate`. We will use Spring DI to initialize the object from XML.

3. We need to change the `addContact()` method to use `JdbcTemplate` to insert the record. The code snippet will be as follows:

   ```
   public int addContact(Contact contact) {
       // TODO Auto-generated method stub
       int record = 0;
       String SQL_INSERT_CONTACT = "insert into Contact_CORE
   values(?,?,?,?,?,?)";
       try{
       record = jdbcTemplate.update(
   ```

```
        SQL_INSERT_CONTACT,
        new Object[] { contact.getFirstName(),
contact.getLastName(),
            contact.getGender(),
contact.getAddress(),
        contact.getEmail(),
contact.getPhone_number() });
    }catch (DuplicateKeyException e) {
        // TODO: handle exception
        e.printStackTrace();
        return 0;
    }
    return record;
}
```

We have not handled any SQL exception as we did in JDBC; this is because, internally, JdbcTemplate will catch any SQL exceptions that are thrown. It will then translate the generic SQL exception into more specific data access exceptions and rethrow it. This exception is an unchecked exception as all Spring's data access exceptions are runtime exceptions. So it's not necessary for us to catch them. Still we are catching them because that is our logical requirement:

1. The controller layer will remain the same as we have already injected ContactDAO in AddController.

2. The configuration file, connection.xml, needs to be changed for the injection and declaration of one more bean of type JdbcTemplate. The JdbcTemplate has a data member of type DataSource. So, while configuring the JdbcTemplate, we need to inject reference of type DataSource. The JdbcTemplate is a data member of ContactDAOImpl. So, while configuring the bean for ContactDAOImpl, the injection of type JdbcTemplate has to be done. The connection.xml will have three beans as follows:

   ° Bean for DataSource

   ° Bean for JdbcTemplate

   ° Bean for ContactDAOImpl. The configuration will be as follows:

   ```
   <bean id="dataSource"
   class="org.springframework.jdbc.datasource.
   DriverManagerDataSource">
     <property name="driverClassName" value="com.mysql.jdbc.
   Driver" />
     <property name="url" value="jdbc:mysql://localhost:3306/
   contactDB" />
     <property name="username" value="root" />
     <property name="password" value="mysql" />
   ```

```
        </bean>

        <bean id="jdbcTemplate"
        class="org.springframework.jdbc.core.JdbcTemplate">
          <property name="dataSource" ref="dataSource"></property>
        </bean>

        <bean id="contactDao"
        class="com.packt.ch04.dao.ContactDAOImpl_Template">
          <property name="jdbcTemplate" ref="jdbcTemplate" />
        </bean>
```

3. Let's deploy the application to check with the data added in the table. The output will be similar to the one which we got while using `DataSource` injection.

Integrating JDBC DAO support

This is dependent upon the DAO design pattern, where the developer writes a class which gets inherited from the `JdbcDaoSupport` class. Getting extended from `DAOSupport` classes has the disadvantage of coupling with the framework.

Let's develop an application to demonstrate how to write an application which uses `DAOSupport` class with the help of the following steps. We will change the same application which we developed for `JdbcTemplate`:

1. Let's change the implementation of `ContactDAOImpl` by extending from `JdbcDAOSupport`. The `JdbcDAOSupport` class provides a `JdbcTemplate` instance which the developer can use. So remove `JdbcTemplate` as data member and its getter and setters.

2. Change the `addContact` to use `JdbcTempate` which has been provided by `JdbcDaoSupport` to insert a record as follows:

```
public int addContact(Contact contact) {
    // TODO Auto-generated method stub
    int record = 0;
    String SQL_INSERT_CONTACT = "insert into Contact_CORE
values(?,?,?,?,?,?)";
    try {
      record = getJdbcTemplate().update(
          SQL_INSERT_CONTACT,
          new Object[] { contact.getFirstName(),
            contact.getLastName(), contact.getGender(),
            contact.getAddress(), contact.getEmail(),
            contact.getPhone_number() });
```

```
        } catch (DuplicateKeyException e) {
          // TODO: handle exception
          e.printStackTrace();
          return 0;
        }
        return record;
      }
```

3. `JdbcTemplate` is not a data member of the `ContactDAOImpl` class but the class is getting extended `JdbcDAOSupport`. So we need to provide the reference of `JdbcTempate` or `DataSource` from the configuration. The `connection.xml` will have the following code snippet:

```
<bean id="dataSource"
class="org.springframework.jdbc.datasource.
DriverManagerDataSource">
    <property name="driverClassName" value="com.mysql.jdbc.Driver"
/>
  <property name="url" value="jdbc:mysql://localhost:3306/
contactDB" />
  <property name="username" value="root" />
  <property name="password" value="mysql" />
</bean>

<bean id="jdbcTemplate" class="org.springframework.jdbc.core.
JdbcTemplate">
  <property name="dataSource" ref="dataSource"></property>
</bean>

<bean id="contactDao" class="com.packt.ch04.dao.ContactDAOImpl">
  <property name="jdbcTemplate" ref="jdbcTemplate" />
</bean>
```

4. The `ContcatController` implementation remains untouched. After deploying and executing the application, we will get one more row added in the `Contact_CORE` table.

We have just seen the ways to handle a database using JDBC basics with the help of Spring integration techniques. The developers don't have to get involved in managing the `Connection`, exception handling and dealing with boilerplate code. For smaller applications, it is fine, but when the application size increases, the pain comes back. Now, as a developer, we need something more. We need something which provides the facility to manage JDBC from the perspective of objects and not SQL-centric.

Problems with JDBC

The problems with JDBC are as follows:

- In JDBC, the developer maps a data member to a table column. This is not object-centric.
- No default mapping is available in JDBC with the table.
- JDBC works using the basics of SQL.
- JDBC uses database-specific code.
- No automatic versioning or timestamping is available.

Introduction to ORM

To overcome these drawbacks, developers have the **Object Relational Mapping (ORM)** technique. ORM helps to manage the impedance mismatch between an object-oriented application and a relational database. ORM helps to write less complex applications. With the help of ORM frameworks, we can persist the objects to the relational tables using the mapping between the tables and the objects. iBatis, JPA and Hibernate are the ORM technologies which are on the market.

Advantages of using ORM

The advantages of using ORM are as follows:

- ORM maps an object to the table
- It supports its own query language instead of using SQL
- Less database-dependent code
- Low maintenance cost
- Optimizes the performance by providing caching
- Provides ways for automatic versioning and timestamping

Let's now discuss the Hibernate framework.

Introduction to Hibernate

Hibernate is a Java-based open source persistence framework also called an ORM tool. It has APIs to support persistence. Hibernate applications define persistence classes that are mapped to the database tables. These persistence classes are POJO classes. POJOs are Plain Old Java Objects, which facilitate holding the data, which makes it easier to send data from one layer to another.

Hibernate architecture

The following diagram shows the core interfaces which are used in Hibernate applications and the interaction of a Java application to access the data from the database using these interfaces through APIs such as JDBC, JTA, or JNDI:

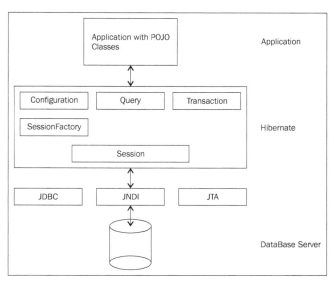

Hibernate architecture

When a developer uses Hibernate, the most important thing is to determine the mapping between the class and the table in the application. This class may be just a POJO or a POJO which supports inheritance or containment. Whatever OOPS strategy the POJO is supporting, there are some facts which the developer needs to always keep in mind:

- The POJO must follow JavaBean specification and must include getter and setter methods.
- If the class exists on its own and if it's not a part of the inheritance or composition strategy, the identifier strategy has to be provided. Hibernate provides different identifier types to generate or built the identifier.

Hibernate internally uses JDBC to connect to the database. Hibernate can be used with an application server where it uses JNDI to handle the connection resource. Hibernate can use a JDBC connection or **Java Transaction API (JTA)** for transaction support.

In Hibernate APIs, there are some important classes and interfaces which the developer commonly comes across:

- `Configuration`: The `Configuration` class is very important in hibernate as it has the responsibility to get the database connection and the mapping for a class to the table:

  ○ To handle the connection, hibernate uses a configuration file which has the name `hibernate.cfg.xml`.

  ○ Hibernate uses mapping files in order to map a class to a table. The name of this file is normally `XXX.hbm.xml`, where XXX will be replaced by the name of the POJO to be mapped. But nowadays, instead of maintaining the file, developers can also use annotations for the mapping.

- `SessionFactory`: It's a singleton, heavyweight class. The `SessionFactory` configures hibernate for application using the configuration file and gives an object of `Session`. As `Sessionfactory` is a heavyweight object, the developer has to take care to use a single object per application.

- `Session`: `Session` is obtained from a `SessionFactory` object. It's needed every time the developer deals with the database to add a new record or to load an existing record from a table. `Session` is lightweight; when it gets instantiated, the connection is made with the database.

- `Query`: The `Query` interface lets the developer query the database, which is completely dependent upon the object identifier.

- `Transaction`: When communication happens between the database and the application, there is a fair chance of something going wrong. This leads to inconsistency on the database side, which may affect the developer's business logic. Transaction supports the development side, helping to maintain integrity.

Let's discuss a small application to get exposure with the hibernate application in the XML way. We will cover mapping using annotation in the next application. We need to do the following steps:

1. Write a POJO whose object we want to persist.

2. Map the POJO in a Hibernate bean mapping file with the name `POJO_name.hbm.xml`. While writing the mapping, provide the identifier strategy and map all the data members with the columns.

3. Write the connection parameters in the `hibernate.cfg.xml` file. Put the file in `classpath` as it's a default location from where hibernate loads the configuration file.

4. Create a class where we write the code to insert the data to the table or to perform other database-related operations.

The steps which need to be performed here will be:

1. Load the configuration file and get an object of `SessionFactory`.
2. From `SessionFactory`, obtain an object of `Session`.
3. Using the object of `Session`, get an object of `Transaction`.
4. Begin the transaction before performing the database operation.
5. Invoke a method on session to perform the database operation.
6. Commit the transaction on successful completion of the database operation. If the operation has failed, rollback the transaction.
7. Close all the resources on completing the operation.

Let's start with development:

1. Create a new Java application with the name `Ch04_Hibernate_Introduction`.

2. Add the following `hibernate` JAR FILES and **mysql-connector-java-5.1.12-bin** jar:

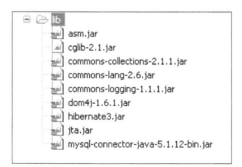

The jar files for hibernate

 You can download the jar from `http://hibernate.org/orm/downloads/`.

3. Create or copy the `Contact` and `Gender` POJO classes following JavaBean specification in the package `com.packt.ch04.pojo`. We have already used these POJOs in previous examples.

4. Create `contact.hbm.xml` to map the bean. While writing the `mapping` file, we need to provide the following information:

   ° This file will contain the tag class which has name and table as attributes. The `name` is the name of POJO which is mapped to the table specified by the attribute `table`.

   ° It has `id` as a tag, which gives an object identifier generation strategy. It must configure `id`.

   ° Each data member in the POJO except the identifier will be mapped by a separate tag `property`.

   ° The configuration file will be as follows:

```xml
<hibernate-mapping>
  <class name="com.packt.ch04.pojo.Contact"table="Contact_
hib">
    <id name="email"type="string">
      <column name="email"/>
      <generator class="assigned"/>
    </id>
    <property name="firstName"type="java.lang.String">
      <column name="FIRST_NAME"/>
    </property>
    <property name="lastName"type="java.lang.String">
      <column name="LAST_NAME"/>
    </property>
    <property name="gender"type="int">
      <column name="GENDER"/>
    </property>
    <property name="address"type="java.lang.String">
      <column name="ADDRESS"/>
    </property>
    <property name="phone_number"type="java.lang.String">
      <column name="PHONENUMBER"/>
    </property>
  </class>
</hibernate-mapping>
```

5. Now create `hibernate.cfg.xml` in the classpath. The configuration file consists of driver class name, URL, username, and password, which helps to obtain a database connection. Along with this, we will configure a few more properties, which are as follows:

   ° `Dialect`: Each database has its own way of firing a query. In Hibernate, the developer is not involved in writing the query; it will be taken care of by the framework. The dialect helps to fire the database-specific query. As we are using a MYSQL database, we are going to use `MySQLDialect`.

   ° `Show_sql`: As hibernate fires the query internally, it's behind the screen. If the developer wants to know what and how a query is fired, we will use this property. This will display the query on the console, making it visible to the developer.

   ° `hbm2ddl.auto`: Hibernate works with tables. It may be possible that the developer wants to create the table every time he is running the application or may want to use existing ones. This property gives information to the framework about what table creation strategy is to be used, such as create, update, create-drop.

   ° `resource`: It specifies which files to load for Hibernate bean mapping.

   The configuration file will be as follows:

```xml
<hibernate-configuration>
  <session-factory>
    <property name="hibernate.connection.driver_class">
      com.mysql.jdbc.Driver
    </property>
    <property name="hibernate.connection.url">
      jdbc:mysql://localhost:3306/contactDB
    </property>
    <property name="hibernate.connection.username">
      root
    </property>
    <property name="hibernate.connection.password">mysql</property>
    <property name="hibernate.dialect">
      org.hibernate.dialect.MySQLDialect
    </property>
    <property name="show_sql">true</property>
    <property name="hbm2ddl.auto">create</property>
    <mapping resource="com/packt/ch04/pojo/Contact.hbm.xml"/>
  </session-factory>
</hibernate-configuration>
```

6. Create an interface `ContactHibernateDao` as the following snippet in `com.packt.ch04.dao` package:

```
public interface ContactHibernateDao {
  String insertContact(Contact contact);
}
```

7. Create the class `ContactHibernateDaoImpl` in the same `dao` package where we use the hibernate API to insert the object of `Contcat` in table. Add `int insertContcat(Contact contact)` for insertion. The code snippet is as follows:

```
public String insertContact(Contact contact) {
    // TODO Auto-generated method stub
    SessionFactorysessionFactory = null;
    Transaction transaction=null;
      Session session=null;
      String email=null;
    try{
    sessionFactory=
new Configuration().configure().buildSessionFactory();
    Session session=sessionFactory.openSession();
    transaction=session.beginTransaction();
    email=(String)session.save(contact);
    transaction.commit();

        }catch (ConstraintViolationException e) {
    // TODO: handle exception
    transaction.rollback();
    e.printStackTrace();
    }
finally{
session.close();
sessionFactory.close();
    }

    return email;
}
```

8. Create the main class from where execution starts. The code snippet will be as follows:

```
public static void main(String[] args) {
    // TODO Auto-generated method stub

    ContactHibernateDao dao=newContactHibernateDaoImpl();
    Contact contact=newContact();
```

```
contact.setEmail("billy@abc.com");
contact.setAddress("Pune");
contact.setFirstName("billy");
contact.setLastName("brown");
contact.setGender(1);
contact.setPhone_number("7876432123");

String email=dao.insertContact(contact);
if(email!=null)
{
System.out.println("data inserted successfully with id:-
"+email);
}
    else {
       System.out.println("please choose new mail ID");
    }

}
```

9. On successful execution, one row will be inserted in the `contact_hib` table. We can check the query which has been fired by Hibernate for insertion of records and the success message on the console as follows:

```
INFO: schema export complete
Hibernate: insert into Contact_hib (FIRST_NAME, LAST_NAME, GENDER, ADDRESS, PHONENUMBER, email) values (?, ?, ?, ?, ?, ?)
Nov 12, 2015 5:24:11 PM org.hibernate.impl.SessionFactoryImpl close
INFO: closing
Nov 12, 2015 5:24:11 PM org.hibernate.connection.DriverManagerConnectionProvider close
INFO: cleaning up connection pool: jdbc:mysql://localhost:3306/contactDB
data inserted successfully with id:- billy@abc.com
```

Hibernate console output

Spring Hibernate integration

Spring provides integration classes so that these ORM technologies can be used depending upon Spring principles. For the integration of Hibernate, Spring provides a class Hibernate template, which has the methods for persisting the object.

Let's redevelop the `Ch04_JdbcTemplate_Integration` application which we developed using `JDBCTemplate` to integrate `HibernateTemplate` in a newly created project `Ch04_Hibernate_Template_Integration`. We will use Hibernate using annotation for the integration with the help of the following steps as we have already seen how to use `xxx.hbm.xml` to map POJO to the table:

1. Add the `.jar` as listed in the following screenshot, which will be for Spring, Hibernate using annotation and MYSQL connector:

The JAR file list for Spring-Hibernate integration.

 We can download the spring jar files from `http://repo.spring.io/release/org/springframework/spring/`.

2. As we want to use annotation-based hibernate mapping, we need to change our `Contact` POJO with mapping annotations and no longer need `Contact.hbm.xml` to map POJO to the database table used in the previous example:

```
@Entity
@Table(name="contact_hib")
public class Contact {
```

```
@NotEmpty
@Length(min=2,max=10)
@Column(name="FIRST_NAME")
private String firstName;

@NotEmpty
@Column(name="LAST_NAME")
private String lastName;

@Column(name="GENDER")
private int gender;

@NotEmpty
@Column(name="ADDRESS")
private String address;

@NotEmpty
@Email(regexp="[A-Za-z0-9._%+-]+@[A-Za-z0-9.-]+\\.[A-Za-z]
{2,4}")
@Id
@Column(name="EMAIL")
private String email;

@NotEmpty
@Pattern(regexp="(^$|[0-9]{10})")
@Column(name="PHONENUMBER")
private String phone_number;
// getters and setters for all the data members.
}
```

The contact will be mapped to the table using the annotation `@Entity`. It maps the class to the table with the same name; in our case, it will be `Contact`. But if we want to map the class with a table having another name then we need to use `@Table` annotation which accepts the name attribute. This name attribute specifies the name of the table with which we want to map the class and each data member which wants to be mapped with the table.

All the data members which we want to map with the columns in the table, we will annotate as `@Column`. The name of the column and the data member will be same. If we want to give something else as the column name then we need to use the name attribute along with `@Column` as we did. We need to add information about @Id also as, the @Id will map the data member to the Primary Key of the table.

3. Instead of using `JdbcTemplate`, we need to declare a data member of type `HibernateTemplate` as follows:

```
HibernateTemplate hibernateTemplate;
```

Add getter and setter for `HibernateTemplate`.

4. Change the `addContact()` method to use `HibernateTemplate` to persist the data using the `persist()` method. The code snippet will be as follows:

```
public int addContact(Contact contact) {
    // TODO Auto-generated method stub
    try {
      hibernateTemplate.persist(contact);
      return 1;
    } catch (DataAccessException e) {
      // TODO: handle exception
      e.printStackTrace();
    }
    return 0;
}
```

5. Let's use DI to inject the `HibernateTemplate` object. Hibernate uses `SessionFactory`. So, while writing the configuration, we need to add a bean for `SessionFactory`. `SessionFactory` needs the connection properties, the class which provides mapping of the POJO to the table, and the dialect, `show_sql`, and `hbm2ddl.auto` properties. The database connection will be provided by the `DataSource` bean so there is no need to provide separate `hibernate.cfg.xml` as we did in the `Hibernate_Introduction` application. Finally, we are going to use `HibernateTemplate` provided by Spring for integration. The configuration `connection.xml` file will look as follows:

```
<bean id="dataSource" class="org.springframework.jdbc.datasource.
DriverManagerDataSource">
    <property name="driverClassName" value="com.mysql.jdbc.Driver"
/>
    <property name="url"
value="jdbc:mysql://localhost:3306/contactDB" />
    <property name="username" value="root" />
    <property name="password" value="mysql" />
</bean>

<bean id="sessionFactory"
  class="org.springframework.orm.hibernate3.annotation.
AnnotationSessionFactoryBean">
    <property name="dataSource" ref="dataSource" />
    <property name="annotatedClasses">
```

```
        <list>
            <value>com.packt.ch04.pojo.Contact</value>
        </list>
    </property>
    <property name="hibernateProperties">
        <props>
            <prop
key="hibernate.dialect">org.hibernate.dialect.MySQLDialect
            </prop>
            <prop key="hibernate.show_sql">true</prop>
            <prop key="hibernate.hbm2ddl.auto">update</prop>
        </props>
    </property>
</bean>

<bean id="hibernateTemplate"
class="org.springframework.orm.hibernate3.HibernateTemplate">
    <property name="sessionFactory" ref="sessionFactory" />
</bean>

<bean id="contactDao" class="com.packt.ch04.dao.ContactDAOImpl">
    <property name="hibernateTemplate" ref="hibernateTemplate" />
</bean>
```

6. On execution, when the user fills in the contact registration form, the data will get inserted in the table `contact_hib` if the e-mail ID is not already available in the database.

7. We specified the database connection related parameters in the `hibernate.cfg.xml` file in the previous example. We will not use this file while doing the integration as the `sessionFactory` object will use `dataSource` for establishing the connection.

8. We will not create the `Contact_hib` manually as we specified `hbm2ddl.auto` to be created while configuring `sessionFactory` for setting hibernate-related properties.

Introduction to unit testing

Unit testing is the process of testing a single functionality in the code at a time. In unit testing, the developer ensures that the functionality is working correctly according to business logic. We will use JUnit for unit testing.

Unit testing using JUnit

JUnit is an automation testing framework which provides numbers of `TestRunners` that can automate the execution of any Java class that extends from `TestCase`. It facilitates the testing of the expected behavior of a method as a unit. The developer can write test cases for all the functions in the code. Whenever a change occurs in the functionality, causing it to behave differently than expected, it can be easily identified and fixed as well. JUnit 4 supports annotation-based programming so instead of getting extended from the `TestCase`, the developer can use annotation-based programming as well.

Steps for writing a TestCase using annotation

Perform the following steps to write a `TestCase`:

1. Create a class `TestCase` by giving a name as `XXXTest` where `XXX` can be replaced by the class under testing. This we called `TestCase`.

2. Create one or more methods for testing a function. Each one of them has to be annotated by `@Test`. The name of this method in general will have a format such as `testXXX_positive()` or `testXX_negative()`, where `XXX` is replaced by the name of the method under testing.

3. In the method, use `assertXXX()` to validate the results of the method under testing according to the expected business logic.

Let's develop a `TestCase` for the code of `dao` layer which we had developed in `Ch04_Hibernate_Template_Integration`using eclipse:

1. The class under testing is `ContactDAOImpl` from the `Ch04_Hibernate_Template_Integration` project.

2. Create a new `TestCase` under `com.packt.ch04.dao.junit` with the name `ContactDAOImplTest`. Select the class under testing as `com.packt.ch04.dao.ContactDAOImpl`. Select `setup()` and `tearDown()` for initializing and releasing the memory. The selection will be as follows:

Creation of a test case using Eclipse

3. Now we need to select the methods which we want to test by clicking on the **Next** button. Select the checkbox of the methods which we want to take under testing. The screenshot will look like this:

Method selection for JUnit testing

We selected `addContact()` for testing. Click on **Finish** to complete the steps. If we are creating the JUnit `TestCase` for the first time in the workspace, we will get a message to **add Junit 4** on the build path as follows:

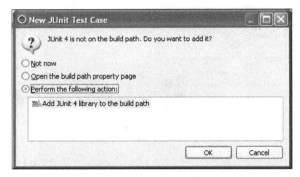

Adding JUnit library to build path

4. Click on **OK** to add the library on the build path.

5. By clicking on the **Finish** button, we have got `TestCase` created from the template.

6. As the object of `ContactDAO` is required in the code and it has to be obtained from the Spring container, we will use a spring API to get an object as follows:

```
@Before
  public void setUp() throws Exception {
    ApplicationContext context=new ClassPathXmlApplicationContext(
"connection.xml");
    dao=(ContactDAO)context.getBean("contactDao");
}
```

7. The object will be set to null to release the memory by garbage collector. The code will be:

```
@After
  public void tearDown() throws Exception {
    dao=null;
}
```

8. While writing the code to test `addContact()`, the argument expected by the method is the `Contact` object. So the first task is to get an object and then pass it to the `addContact()` method. Now it's time to test using `assertXXX()` as per the return type of the method under testing. The code snippet will be:

```
@Test
  public void testAddContact() {
```

```
Contact contact=new Contact();
contact.setEmail("abcde@abc.com");
contact.setAddress("Waecity");
contact.setFirstName("billy");
contact.setLastName("brown");
contact.setPhone_number("3456543129");

int record=dao.addContact(contact);
assertEquals(1,record );
}
```

9. It's always better to be on the safe side when carrying out positive as well as negative testing. The previous code is about positive testing where we got the code successfully executed by inserting a new record in the table. Now we will do negative testing to insert the same record which we did in the previous code. This time we will get no record added as e-mail ID acts as primary key. The code snippet will be as follows:

```
@Test
  public void testAddContact_Negative() {

    Contact contact=new Contact();
    contact.setEmail("abcd89@abc.com");
    contact.setAddress("Waecity");
    contact.setFirstName("billy");
    contact.setLastName("brown");
    contact.setPhone_number("3456543129");

    int record=dao.addContact(contact);
    assertEquals(0,record );
  }
```

10. Now select the **TestCase** and run it as **JUnit Test** as shown in the following screenshot:

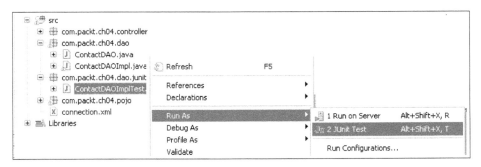

Running a JUnit test case

11. On successful execution, we will get the output from JUnit view as follows:

JUnit execution output

In the same way, we can develop the code for finding all the records or finding a record by using mail ID from the database. The complete code along with JUnit testing can be referred to in the project Ch04_Hibernate_Template_Integration.

Summary

When we write down an application, it needs to deal with information and data taken from the real world. Along with processing the accepted data, we also need to use this data for future purposes with the help of the persistence layer. The goal of this chapter was to provide different techniques and ways of storing data permanently. Here we have covered most of the techniques to save the data in database tables using Spring. We've covered JDBC overview, mapping data using Hibernate and the integration of these techniques in Spring. Instead of giving a full stop to development, here we moved a step ahead and carried out JUnit testing to find out how the code is actually behaving for a certain set of data.

In the next chapter, we will learn how to develop the most important layer of an application—the business layer—and about communication between the layers.

5
Developing the
Business Layer

In every application, there are a number of components available. Some deal with user interfaces, some deal with the database, and some deal with configuration. But the core component which will decide how to deal with data is the business component. The business component will be involved in handling the data with immense care so that there will not be any mess; neither on the data side nor on the application flow side. The responsibility of these components is to manipulate the data by applying some mathematical formulae and certain business rules. These components will be involved in taking all kinds of decisions for handling the data to and fro in the application.

The application will have multiple layers that comprise of presentation, data storage, and business logic handling. The **data access object** (**DAO**) layer and the presentation layer are involved in adding data to the database layers and accepting data from the user respectively. Both of these layers are involved in the handling of data. These layers are not about what the logical part is, what the decision is, or how manipulation of data will be done. These layers are not taking part in any decision-making nor in deciding which module will come next in the flow. Nowhere have they checked whether the data is getting inserted, updated, and whether they have removed the correct layer or not. This scenario leads to problems such as maintaining the consistency of data, applying a wrong business formula, invoking a wrong module, data getting updated in one table but not in another, and many more. That means, ultimately, the application fails in the market. It's the developer's responsibility to develop the correct flow in an application which will fulfill the business logic correctly. They need to understand the business flow and accordingly, build up the modules which will communicate with each other and give the right solution to the problem. If they get the business logic incorrect then there will be a blunder when the application executes.

Both the layers which we already discussed in the previous two chapters have their own responsibilities to perform. This is the point where we need to discuss the most important layer: the business layer. Transaction management is one such concern of the business logic. Transaction management helps developers to maintain the consistency of the data with the help of commit or rollback methods. In the same manner, there are many other ways to maintain the logical part of the project.

In this chapter, we will discuss the following topics:

- How to implement the business layer
- How to communicate with the business layer
- How to wrap up the layers to collaborate

Business logic

Let's discuss what exactly business logic is, in a simplified manner with a few scenarios:

- **Scenario 1**: Let's take a very simple banking example. The common operations which a bank holder does are the deposit and withdrawal of money. Every bank has certain rules for the maintenance of a minimum balance. The account holder cannot withdraw an amount below this minimum balance. We also need to remember here that every bank has their set of rules about what will be the minimum balance, for example, SBI has 500 Rupees, HDBC and ICICI have 5,000 Rupees, and so on. The minimum balance of an account is also dependent upon what type of account you have: for example, salary accounts can be zero balance accounts. Again, these rules change from bank to bank as a part of their business policy and their tie-ups with companies. In the persistence layer, the developers will develop the code so that after every withdrawal, the updated balance, the withdrawal amount, and other details of the transaction will be stored in the database table. But here they also have to follow the minimum balance rule in order to make sure that no one will be able to withdraw an amount if the minimum balance has reached its limit. They will do this by checking the minimum balance and the type of account every time before a withdrawal.

- **Scenario 2**: Let's discuss a second scenario. Every bank has a number of users specifically divided into two main categories of bank account: savings accounts and current accounts. The savings account holders take advantage of the interest rates on their balance offered by banks. But the current account holder doesn't have such a facility. At the end of the financial year, every bank gives yearly interest to account holders. This interest has to be calculated depending upon the type of account and the amount in the account.

This can also depend on the deposit and withdrawal transactions made on the account. So, while calculating the interest, all these things have to be carefully considered.

The interest gets calculated for fixed deposits as well. All banks provide a facility of fixed deposit to customers. The interest rate varies as per bank norms depending on the deposit amount, duration of deposit, and the depositor's age. When a developer develops such modules, they have to think about multiple scenarios where the rules and formulas will be dependent upon certain scenarios. This is about normal conditions but sometimes the account holder wants to withdraw the fixed deposit before the term ends as well. Only, accepting data from the user and adding it to the table will not complete the process flow, but along with accepting data, it should be again processed depending upon the above-discussed conditions.

- **Scenario 3**: We will discuss one more scenario based on railway reservations. At the time of railway reservations, we select a particular train and date of travel. We check for the availability of seats and start the process of booking the ticket. When the process of booking starts, a few available seats are shown to us. We then select the seat and now we are in the mode of payment, which may take too much time. Meanwhile, all the available tickets have been booked by other passengers and no seat is available. Being unaware that the seats are not available, we complete the payment process. Thus, instead of getting confirmed tickets, we lose the money and do not have the booking as well. We get frustrated as a user because the payment has already been done and we cannot undo that. We cannot undo that as a user, but as part of the development, the developers had already thought of such situation and have developed a module for reverting the transaction done by you by reversing the booking. Actually, booking and transferring the money is the developer's task, but along with the booking, the developer needs to think about successful and unsuccessful bookings as well. In the case of successful bookings, the user should get the booking details. If the booking is unsuccessful, the respective message should be shown on the UI. The developers also have to think about transferring the money to the railway on success or vice versa on an unsuccessful activity. Where the money gets transferred correctly is a part of business logic.

All of the above discussed scenarios prove the significance of developing the correct business logic and writing it for the appropriate situations. And if this module fails, the whole business will collapse. Developing the business logic is simple as well as complicated. It is simple because the formulas and decisions to be made are already known to you as a developer; it is difficult because to apply the rule, we first need to know the domain for which we are developing the application, you should have a correct process knowledge and, last but not least, you should be aware of the rules to be applied. Simply, there is no hard and fast rule—everything is dependent!

When someone wants to develop any kind of business layer, there are multiple things which need to be considered, understood, and kept in mind with immense care. Most of us feel that developing the business layer is difficult. Most of the time, it is hard just because of the lack of knowledge and we don't know from where to start and how to start.

Domain knowledge

While discussing why domain knowledge is important, we discussed many scenarios. In each scenario, we used a number of technical terms, such as minimum balance, interest rate, fixed deposits, savings account, reservation, bookings, and many more. Much of this terminology is used in our day-to-day life; some of it is not quite frequently in use but we are aware of it. When a team starts in any field, such as banking, reservation, travelling, and insurance, they need to understand the basic terms used in the respective field. They need to understand their importance and when to use what. They should have conditional knowledge of the situations as well.

Acquiring expertise and thorough knowledge of a certain area, industry from in and out is domain knowledge. Some examples of domain knowledge are:

*   Knowledge of accounting systems, steps and procedures
*   Knowledge of life insurance
*   Knowledge of the tax sector
*   Knowledge of the manufacturing industry
*   E-commerce knowledge

Getting domain knowledge is a time-consuming task. Those who are interested in getting domain knowledge can refer to the documentation available online or in many books and reference material. The person also has to not only study each point theoretically, but they have to also apply it to real examples. One of the best ways to get domain knowledge is through case studies. We can also get domain knowledge from group discussions. But when we get involved in group discussions, we need to have some basic knowledge to understand what is going on. In all such fruitful group discussions, the experts can share their past experiences.

Rules, formulas, and conditions

Domain knowledge gives us information about situations, the rules which need to be considered in those situations, situation-based formulae, and conditional-based decision making. For example, in interest calculation, we consider the account type, and in reservation booking, we need to know the number of seats, type of carriage, and age of the passengers. Before starting the actual work, it's always better to put all rules dependent on situations, and formulae to apply on certain cases together that is well understood from knowledge or by discussions. All the situations where the flow of an application can fail or should not flow unless being corrected are called exceptional situations; for example, the user gives a withdrawal option while there is no sufficient balance, and the user chooses to buy a product which is not in stock. All such exceptional conditions need to be known to the developers as well as to the testers. The developers and testers consider these situations while developing and testing the applications respectively.

Case studies

Reading books, papers, and magazines will certainly help to get knowledge of how a particular industry works and what the important terminologies and conditions are. But it will not be sufficient as this acquired knowledge needs to be applied in reality. With the help of a case study, a situation can be well understood and we come to know the loopholes in it, why that situation occurred, and how to come out of it. As a case study is situation-based, it helps the developer a lot as they can relate it to the application flow.

A case study gives a practical solution which can be applied in the application directly. It may not be possible to modify the solution as per the requirement. The case study helps to grab domain knowledge relatively in a quick and easy way.

Developing the business layer

After a long, theoretical discussion, let's now develop the business layer for the code which we developed in the previous chapter for contact management. We need to set the rules which can be applied in our contact management project.

The following is the rule to be applied:

- A contact will be successfully inserted only when there is no pre-registration of the e-mail in the table. We have already developed code where `DuplicateEntryExeption` has been handled. This exception handling helps the developer to understand that no duplicate contact has been entered in the table. We can do this manually as well as using database basics. If we want to do it manually, then we first need to fetch all the records from the contact table and cross-check whether the email entered by the user is already existing or not. We can make this simply by putting email as a primary key in the database. So whenever the user enters an email which already exists, an exception will be thrown.

Let's redevelop the `Ch04_JdbcTemplate_Integration` application as `Ch05_contact_management_case1` using the following steps:

1. First of all, we will add the business logic layer to provide implementation of the business logic of checking whether the user is entering a duplicate number or not. We will do the duplication check by adding the interface with business methods for adding the contact.
2. Then we will check whether the data already exists or not.
3. If it doesn't exist then we will add it, otherwise we will return a message.

Let's start the code development:

1. Add a method in `ContactDAO` interface which we already used in all the previous examples as `int findContactToAdd(String email)`.
2. Implement it in `ContactDAOImpl` to find out if there are any records available with the same email. This is done as follows:

```
public int findContactToAdd(String email)
  {
    String sql = "select COUNT(*) from Contact_CORE where
email=?";
    return jdbcTemplate.queryForInt(sql,email);
  }
```

3. Add an interface `ContactBussiness` in `com.packt.ch05.bussiness` package as follows:

```
public interface ContactBussiness {
  int addContact(Contact contact);
}
```

4. Implement it in `ContactBussinessImpl`, but while implementing this we need to understand a few things. The first one is, now the controller will not be interacting with the DAO layer but it will interact with the business layer and the business layer will interact with the DAO. So the class should have an object of `ContactDAO`. This will be possible with `@Autowired`. In order to manage the object of `ContactBussnessImpl` by the Spring container, we have added `@Component` annotation. The `@Component` will give us the advantage of getting an object of the class whose lifecycle will be managed by the Spring container without configuring the `XXX.xml` file (in our case `connection.xml`), that is, its replacement of the following configuration:

```
<bean id=" " class=""/>
```

When we use `@Component` by default, the value of `id` is `contactBussinessImpl`, which is the decapitalized name of the class. If we want a different value of `id`, we need to add an attribute named `value`. Now we don't have to configure it in the XML file. `checkContact(Contact contact)` will check whether the email already exists or not. As only `ContactBussinessImpl` needs it, we will make this method private:

```
@Component(value="contactBussiness")
public class ContactBussinessImpl implements ContactBussiness {
  @Autowired
  ContactDAO contactDAO;
public int addContact(Contact contact) {
    // TODO Auto-generated method stub
    if(checkContact(contact))
    {
      return contactDAO.addContact(contact);
    }
    return 0;


  }
Private boolean checkContact(Contact contact)
  {
    if(contactDAO.findContactToAdd(contact.getEmail())==0)
    {
      return true;
    }
    return false;
  }
}
```

5. Let's update `AddController`. Take out the following code:

```
@Autowired
  ContactDAO contactDAO;
```

6. Add the code of integrating `ContactBussiness` as follows:

```
 @Autowired
ContactBussiness contactBussiness;
```

7. Modify the code of the `addController` method as follows:

```
int record = contactBussiness.addContact(contact);
```

This replaces the following code:

```
int record = contactDAO.addContact(contact);
```

We are done with the development of the business logic layer. Let's execute the application. After executing the code, if we enter an already existing email, the output will be as shown in the following screenshot:

Contact Registration

FIRST NAME abc
LAST NAME abc
GENDER M
ADDRESS mumbai
PHONE NUMBER 2345123454
EMAIL abc@gmail.com
Add Contact
Data Cannot be inserted Email is already registered

As we have already discussed in earlier chapters, the layering mechanism provides a facility to write down code separated in multiple layers. But they can still collaborate with each other with the help of DI and form one flow within an application. The business layer is invoking the methods of the DAO layer, and the methods of the business layer are invoked from the UI layer. To achieve collaboration, each layer needs to invoke the methods of another. That means they need the object of another class. It's clear from the code that we have made objects available using DI. DI makes objects available for the code as well as helping in achieving the abstraction.

As we have used separation of work using layers, it is easy to change any layer without affecting another. If, for example, today developers are using MySQL and tomorrow they want to use Oracle, the developers don't need to change anything in the business layer. They just have to add a new class which will deal with Oracle and a few changes in the configuration. We have just discussed a very basic scenario of duplication of contact numbers. We can still extend the application by providing a few more operations. We can have a mechanism for updating the contact information from time to time. To achieve this and to make sure only authenticated users will be able to update information, we need to provide credentials. The username will be the email of the user and the password will be the firstname. The password can be updated later by the user. So the information will get updated in two tables: first where we added the user contact details and second in the credentials table.

Both of the above situations can be managed by either of the following methods:

- A solution where the developer will first cross-check whether the email entered by the user is already registered and inform the user

- Using transaction management, where if data is not entered in one table, it will not be entered in another

Let's now discover how to use transaction management in our application. But before discussing transaction management in Spring, first we will discuss transaction management in general and also how we do transaction management using Java.

Transaction management

There are many times when in an application we need to fire multiple queries of add, update, remove, or all of them as a batch. In a batch of statements where multiple queries get fired against a database as a unit, all the queries should be successful or none of them. This is called transaction management. Transaction management is helpful in maintaining data consistency. In transaction management, it is not necessary that the queries should be fired against different tables in a database.

The following are the properties of a transaction:

- **Atomicity**: When firing multiple queries, either all of them should be committed or none of them. This property makes sure that whatever operations are performed on the database and whenever any error occurs, no operations will be performed on the database.

- **Consistency**: Before and after completing the transaction, the state of all the tables will be consistent. If any error occurs, the state of every table may vary. This leads to variable states of the tables. In order to maintain the states of all the tables as unique, whatever data has been changed has to be returned to the original state.

- **Isolation**: It may be possible that in each application there are occurrences of multiple transactions that involve read, write, or update operations. So the transaction which is in progress must be separated from the one which is committed.

- **Durability**: The data which we try to write or update in the table may fail partially. This leads to incorrect states of the tables. Durability makes sure that whenever any operation fails, the data will be available in the correct state.

JDBC and transaction management

In JDBC, transactions are automatically committed. In order to implement transactions in JDBC, we need to add the following steps:

1. We need to invoke `setAutoCommit(false)` on a connection object.

2. Whenever all the operations on the database complete, invoke `commit()`.

3. If any error occurs, invoke `rollback()` to get back to the original state of the table.

Spring and transaction management

Spring provides a transaction management API which aims to provide an alternative to EJB transaction management. Spring provides support for both declarative as well as programmatic transaction management. Spring has the following two types of transaction:

- **Local transactions**: Local transactions are useful when resources are managed at a single point which involves a local transaction manager. JDBC is one such example which handles local transaction which is easy to use and manage. But local transactions cannot handle multiple transaction resources.

- **Global transactions**: Global transactions are useful in distributed systems where resources are distributed at multiple locations with the help of application servers through **Java Transaction API (JTA)**. In order to manage global transactions, JNDI is configured in the server which is used by the developer.

Spring is not managing the transaction management directly, but it gives flexibility to choose transaction management implementation according to the platform. Some of the transaction managers are as shown in the following diagram:

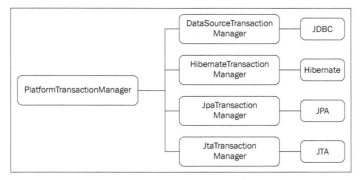

Transaction managers

Let's now discover how to integrate `TransactionManager` in our application. As we are dealing with plain JDBC in `JdbcTemplate`, we will configure the `DataSourceTransaction` manager which provides good support. Also, we need to know the different ways that are available to manage transactions. The following two ways are used to manage transactions:

- Programmatic transactions
- Declarative transactions

Programmatic transaction

In programmatic transaction, the developer manages the transaction through coding. The use of programmatic transaction provides fine control and flexibility to manage operations as the operation is under the control of the developer. Developers can define the rules of managing the transaction and are able to decide the boundaries to decide where to start and where to complete the transaction.

Declarative transaction

Contrary to programmatic transaction, the developer will not code a lot in source code but it will be configured in the XML file. It gives convenience but less precise control. Let's discuss it in depth.

Managing declarative transaction in Spring

Transaction management is one of the very famous cross-cutting technologies. Spring provides **Aspect Oriented Programming (AOP)** to manage cross-cutting technologies. AOP will be used for managing declarative transactions as well.

The transaction is centered around advice which gets called before as well as after the annotated business logic method with the help of the implemented class `TransactionInterceptor`. The before aspect decides the scope of the database transaction, such as keeping the ongoing transaction or creating a new transaction. The after aspects decide to commit or rollback the transaction.

The transaction manager needs to decide to start a new or keep an ongoing transaction continued at the time of transaction before advice. This decision is taken with the help of the propagation attribute. Whenever any business logic method is called by the developer the method of the proxy object gets called.

Let's discuss how to develop transaction management step-by-step.

Step 1

Decide the transaction attributes:

- **Propagation behavior**: Propagation behavior gives an idea of what to do with the transaction when one method call gets propagated. It tells whether to start a new transaction for the called method by suspending what is available, pass on the same transaction further, and to support or not to support the transaction.

  The following table lists propagation behaviors and their meaning:

Propagation behavior	Meaning
PROPAGATION_MANDATORY	Indicates that the method must run within a transaction. If no existing transaction is in progress, an exception will be thrown.
PROPAGATION_NESTED	Indicates that the method should be run within a nested transaction if an existing transaction is in progress.
PROPAGATION_NEVER	Indicates that the current method shouldn't run within a transactional context. If an existing transaction is in progress, an exception will be thrown.
PROPAGATION_NOT_SUPPORTED	Indicates that the method shouldn't run within a transaction. If an existing transaction is in progress, it'll be suspended for the duration of the method.

Propagation behavior	Meaning
PROPAGATION_REQUIRED	Indicates that the current method must run within a transaction. If an existing transaction is in progress, the method will run within that transaction.
PROPAGATION_REQUIRES_NEW	Indicates that the current method must run within its own transaction.
PROPAGATION_SUPPORTS	Indicates that the current method doesn't require a transactional context, but may run within a transaction if one is already in progress.

- **Isolation level**: It's a possibility that at any one time, many transactions are started by the application as it supports concurrency. The isolation level defines the effect of one transaction on another in order to reflect the updated data. This leads to some famous problems, such as the following:

    ◦ **Dirty reads**: Let's consider a situation where two users are using the XXX table. The first user reads the data and has a set of values which are there in the table at this moment, say, for example, 10 records. The second user is adding two new records, but has not yet committed them. The first user can read their data, which is a new set which says they have 12 records and not 10. If all goes well, no problem. Both are happy. But if at the time of record insertion by the second user, he has some problem and it gets rolled back then the first user has 12 records and in the actual table, there are just 10.

    ◦ **Phantom read**: Suppose the first user tries to read data depending upon some criteria. They discover no record matches the criteria. The second user meanwhile inserts or updates a record which matches the first user's searching criteria. If the first user re-executes the query with the same criteria, surprisingly he finds a match.

    ◦ **Non-repeatable reads**: In this scenario, a transaction reads the data twice. But in the first read and in the second, the data read is different. The first user reads a table and gets the values in transaction. The second user deletes or updates rows by transaction. Now the first user again reads the data. They will discover that there is no such row available or the values obtained this time are different than they read earlier.

The possible isolations are as follows:

Isolation level	Meaning
ISOLATION_DEFAULT	Uses the default isolation level of the underlying datastore.
ISOLATION_READ_UNCOMMITTED	Allows you to read changes that haven't yet been committed. May result in dirty reads, phantom reads, and non-repeatable reads.
ISOLATION_READ_COMMITTED	Allows reads from concurrent transactions that have been committed. Dirty reads are prevented, but phantom and non-repeatable reads may still occur.
ISOLATION_REPEATABLE_READ	Multiple reads of the same field will yield the same results, unless changed by the transaction itself. Dirty reads and non-repeatable reads are prevented, but phantom reads may still occur.
ISOLATION_SERIALIZABLE	This fully ACID-compliant isolation level ensures that dirty reads, non-repeatable reads, and phantom reads are all prevented. This is the slowest of all isolation levels because it's typically accomplished by doing full table locks on the tables involved in the transaction.

- **Read-only**: Sometimes the developers are interested in only reading the underlying data and they want to avoid modification of the data. To apply a read-only attribute, the propagation should be one of the following: PROPAGATION_REQUIRED, PROPAGATION_NESTED, and PROPAGATION_REQUIRES_NEW.
- **Transaction timeout**: Some transactions take more time to complete, which hampers performance. In such situations, instead of waiting for a long time, it's better to terminate it. A transaction timeout attribute helps to terminate such time-consuming transactions automatically after a certain time. To apply a timeout attribute, the propagation should be one of the following: PROPAGATION_REQUIRED, PROPAGATION_NESTED, or PROPAGATION_REQUIRES_NEW.

In an application, it may be possible that the process will take more time due to loading of large data from a database or some coding errors of unending loops. In such situations, the client needs to wait for the application to load. The developer will specify the value of the timeout attribute in order to manage after how much time the transaction should be rolled back automatically:

- **Rollback rules**: Normally rollback happens on occurrences of runtime exceptions. But we can define the rules of when to roll back as well as checked and unchecked exceptions. It's also possible to define the rule of specific exceptions and when not to do a transaction rollback.

Step 2

Decide whether you want to adapt declarative transaction or programmatic transaction. If you decide on declarative transaction, take a quick decision to go with XML-based transaction configuration or annotation-based transaction. We will go with declarative transaction using annotation.

Step 3

Due to the problems faced by using the `TransactionProxyFactoryBean` bean in earlier versions of Spring, now Spring comes with namespace `tx`, which can be configured and used to simplify declarative transaction using annotation:

```
<tx:annotation-driven transaction-manager="transactionManager" />
```

The preceding configuration will be configured in order to know which transaction manager handles the operations. This configuration enables Spring to find out all those beans which have been applied with the `@Trasactional` annotation. Now all these beans will be advised with transaction advice. All transaction-related attributes can be defined for `@Transactional` as parameters.

Declarative transaction management

Let's redevelop the application which we just developed in this chapter for case 1 using declarative transaction management as `Ch05_JdbcTemplate_Transaction_Declarative`:

1. Declare a new interface `ContactBussiness` in the `com.packt.ch05.bussiness` package.

2. Implement it in `ContactBussinessImpl`.

    We will concentrate on two methods: `addContact()` and `checkContact()`. The `addContact()` method is expected to add the data to the database so that it should come under transaction management and it should not be read-only. So we will start with `@Transactional(readOnly = false)`. In the same way, `checkContact()` will also be considered for transactions but as this method is involved in only reading the data from the table, it should not be allowed to change it. That means this method should have the following annotation: `@Transactional(readOnly = true)`.

The code snippet will be as follows:

```
@Transactional(readOnly = false)
  public int addContact(Contact contact) {
    // TODO Auto-generated method stub
    if (checkContact(contact)) {
      return contactDAO.addContact(contact);
    }
    return 0;
}

@Transactional(readOnly = true)
private boolean checkContact(Contact contact) {
  if (contactDAO.findContactToAdd(contact.getEmail()) == 0) {
    return true;
  }
  return false;
}
```

There will not be any changes in underlying layers. Now it's time to configure the transaction manager in the XML file.

3. In order to tell Spring to examine all the beans annotated with `@Transactional`, we just need to configure a single line as follows:

    ```
    <tx:annotation-driven/>
    ```

    Here, by default, Spring will search for a bean with `id = "transactionManager"`. So there has to be one more bean, declared with the following configuration:

    ```
    <bean id="transactionManager"
      class="org.springframework.jdbc.datasource.
    DataSourceTransactionManager">
        <property name="dataSource"ref="dataSource"/>
      </bean>
    ```

    As we are using JDBC, we have used `DataSourceTrasactionManger` here.

Sometimes we do have to configure more than one transaction manager or we don't want to use some other value for the ID of the transaction manager; in such cases, we can specify transaction-manager as an attribute to tell which transaction manager is to be used. It can be done as follows:

```
<tx:annotation-driven transaction-manager="transactionManager1"/>
```

If we are using the preceding configuration then we need to declare the configuration as follows:

```
<bean id="transactionManager1"
    class="org.springframework.jdbc.datasource.
DataSourceTransactionManager">
    <property name="dataSource" ref="dataSource"/>
</bean>
```

The preceding configuration gives us a facility to use more than one transaction manager for an application. We are ready to use the application which is taking advantage of transaction management.

Programmatic transaction management

In the previous discussion, we discussed declarative transaction, where the developer has least control. There are two ways in which a developer can opt to go for programmatic transaction:

- Using a transaction template
- Using PlatformTransactionManager

Let's redevelop the application using programmatic transaction, which gives the facility of having fine control. We will use the application which we developed in this chapter for case 1 using declarative transaction management using PlatformTransactionManager:

1. Declare a new interface ContactBussiness in the com.packt.ch05.bussiness package in Ch05_JdbcTemplate_Transaction_Programmatic, which is an extension of Ch04_JdbcTemplate_Integration. You can use the application which we just developed for declarative transaction management. You just need to change the implementation of ContactBussinessImpl as discussed in the following steps.

2. Implement it in ContactBussinessImpl. Declare PlatformTransactionManager as a data member which we will inject using the @Autowired annotation as shown in the following code:

```
@Autowired
    PlatformTransactionManager transactionManager;
```

3. In the `addContact(Contact contact)` method, get an instance of `TransactionDefination`. Use this instance to obtain an instance of `TransactionStatus`. Whenever the operation of adding contacts to the database gets completed, commit the operation. The code will be as follows:

```
public int addContact(Contact contact) {
    // TODO Auto-generated method stub
    TransactionDefinition definition=new
DefaultTransactionDefinition();
    TransactionStatus status=transactionManager.
getTransaction(definition);
    if (checkContact(contact)) {
        transactionManager.commit(status);
        return contactDAO.addContact(contact);
    }

    return 0;
}
```

`PlatformTransactionManager` gives an abstract way to define transaction strategy. It can be stubbed or mocked as necessary to use in programmatic transaction as we did. We configured `DataSourceTransactionManger`, which has been injected in the object of `BussinessImpl`. It has the `getTransaction()` method, which returns an instance of `TransactionStatus`. `TransactionStatus` which is a representation of the transaction status. `TransactionStatus` will be used to obtain status information and to commit or rollback the transaction as follows:

```
transactionManager.commit(status);
```

The `getTransaction()` method gives the status depending upon the `TransactionDefination` instance. The `TransactionDefination` instance has methods to set transaction attributes such as isolation level, propagation, and timeout.

4. We need to change `findContact()` to use transaction management. In `findContact()`, we need to use the `readOnly` policy as here we don't want to have any change in the database. The `readOnly` method is available on `DefaultTransactionDefination`. The code will be as follows:

```
public Contact findContact(String email) {
    // TODO Auto-generated method stub
    TransactionDefinition definition=newDefaultTransactionDefiniti
on();
```

```
    ((DefaultTransactionDefinition)definition).setReadOnly(true);
    TransactionStatus status=transactionManager.
getTransaction(definition);
    return contactDAO.findContact(email);
}
```

Depending upon the situation, the developer decides when to commit the data and when to rollback. The developer can decide the transaction attributes and can change them as per the requirements. It gives fine control on the transaction as opposed to declarative transaction.

How to choose a transaction management strategy is a question of debate as it depends upon the situation and process flow. But whenever developers want to choose between programmatic transaction and declarative transaction, they need to think of how finely they want to handle transactions. If the requirement is to have fine control over transaction management, then they need to choose programmatic transaction. If you also want to keep your code clean and don't want to get involved in coding, use declarative transaction.

Summary

Data is collected from the user through the UI; it is handled using the DAO layer but when to insert and how to insert is decided by the business logic layer. In this chapter, we have discussed the parameters such as market rules, situations to be taken care of, and transaction management to set up business rules. We discussed the way Spring handles transaction management using AOP. We demonstrated how to handle declarative transaction management and how to make transaction management more effective with the help of transaction attributes such as isolation level, timeout, or read-only.

Here we have completed the development of all layers. We have also done JUnit testing of the DAO layer. In this chapter, we have looked at the collaboration of layers. If there is code, there is a possibility of melting the code down. This leads to testing of the give and take between two layers.

In the next chapter, we will talk about testing the collaboration between the layers, and the integration testing. We will discuss what integration testing is, why we need it and, most importantly, how to do integration testing.

6
Testing Your Application

Any application which has completed its development will proceed to the next step of verifying whether the application is actually working. This phase is very important as it is where we ensure the correctness of the product and try to find any flaws in development which may have been overlooked at the time of writing the code. This phase is technically called testing. But now the meaning, implementation, and importance have been changed a lot. We are going to explore testing, the involvement of testing in writing good code, the role of the developer in testing, and much more.

In this chapter, we are going to explore the following topics:

- What is testing?
- The different phases involved in testing an application
- How to test JavaEE applications
- The use of JUnit/Mockito//
- Introduction to Arqullian testing

Software testing

An application is the solution to a problem proposed by the client. In providing the solution, the developer provides an implementation depending upon some rules and algorithms. They concentrate on providing a correct implementation to achieve the appropriate level of quality, which meets the client requirement in all aspects. The developed application must be verified to ensure that it meets the correct requirement and specifications. The process of verifying, to prove that the product is working correctly, is more precisely called; software testing.

Software testing cannot guarantee that the application is high-quality software, but it ensures that the application will operate in a given manner based on the values provided to it. It finds the flaws in the application but doesn't guarantee their absence. We always need to remember that testing of an application is always dependent upon the values which the tester is going to provide. So if a tester fails to judge the condition, the application will be tested but with the wrong values.

Let's not directly move into the details of how to do testing and other such details. First of all, let's get an overview of the application development lifecycle. This discussion will be helpful for understanding the way testing has been changed and the importance of it as well.

Each application development lifecycle is roughly divided into problem analysis, designing the solution for the problem, implementing the design, testing the implementation, and deploying the module. Traditionally, the waterfall model was used for software development.

The waterfall model

In the waterfall model, each step must be completed before you start the next step. In the waterfall model, understanding the problem is the most important factor in order to design it correctly. The risks and problems emerge in the later stages of the process, which is the drawback of this model.

The following diagram illustrates the flow of the waterfall model:

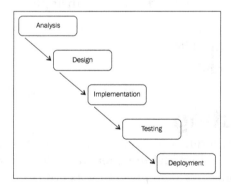

When the application is small, it is easy to adopt such a model but if the application is large, each step takes a long time to complete. As testing comes at the end, whether the requirements of the client have been met by the developed solutions or not comes to our notice at a very late stage, which is a high risk. In the worst situations, the solution may fail completely. Efforts have been made to overcome the drawbacks of the waterfall model in the spiral model.

The spiral model

The following diagram illustrates the flow of the Spiral model:

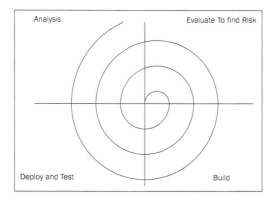

In the spiral model, the entire lifecycle is divided into small spans in contrast to the waterfall model which takes a long time. It's mostly associated with **Rapid Application Development (RAD)**. It gives a facility to receive early customer feedback to spot the problem and meet the exact requirement. As the requirement analysis is on a regular basis, changes can be incorporated more easily. One of the drawbacks faced in adopting this model is its difficulty to manage. In order to overcome this drawback, the spiral model has been logically extended to iterative models.

The V model

The V model is considered an extension of the waterfall model and is in a V shape. Actually, the name V is not just because of its V shape but because of two famous terms used in the model: **Verify** and **Validate**. The following diagram illustrates the V model:

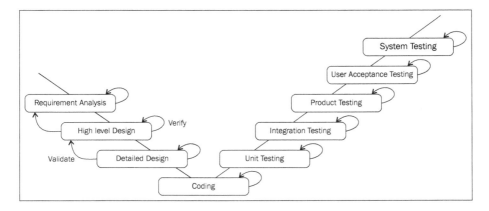

Verification phases

Verification finds out whether the requirements are understood correctly or not. The verification phases are as follows:

- **Requirement analysis**: This phase collects the client requirements in order to understand their expectations. The acceptance test is written depending upon this phase. The requirements collected from the client are used as the input in the acceptance test.

- **High-level design**: After client requirement gathering, now it is time to take decisions about the hardware and software to be used in development.

- **Detailed design**: In this phase, detailed designing of each module is done. It's a very important phase to make the design of each module in such a way that it will be compatible with other modules. It will be used rigorously in the coding or implementation phase. After implementing, it is very important to check whether each module is working in the expected way or not. Faults and errors are caught by unit testing. This is a perfect time to design unit tests based on detailed design.

Validation phases

Validation helps in finding whether the requirements which we understood are correct or not from the previous phase. The validation phases are as follows:

- **Unit testing**: Unit testing is performed on a unit to find out whether it is working as per expectations or not. Unit test cases will be written on the basis of test cases which give a detailed description about what scenarios are to be considered while writing the JUnit test case. As a unit test is concentrated and executed on a module, errors and flaws in the module can be caught at a very early stage and can be removed easily.

- **Integration testing**: Integration testing tests the integration or communication of two modules.

- **Product testing**: In product testing, each and every functionality as per the requirement is checked.

- **Acceptance testing**: This testing is used to find out whether each and every requirement which has been put forward by the client has been fulfilled or not. It's done in the client environment. Along with business logic, the presentation is also tested rigorously.

- **System testing**: In system testing, the communication with the system and compatibility with the platform is tested.

After having a long discussion, we have now well understood the lifecycle of an application. If we apply the V model in our contact management application, we can conclude that we have already finished the development phase. If we recollect, we have also done JUnit testing of the modules. We have developed the business logic layer in the previous chapter. That means now it's time to go ahead with integration testing. But we haven't yet done unit testing of the controller and the business layer as well. Testing the data layer was easy for us because we had access to the data layer. For a while, let's assume we don't have a database and we are developing the data layer. Along with development, testing has to be done. But we can't do that as there is no database. We cannot test! Actually, no. There are many times in development when the code a developer is developing is dependent on environmental factors, such as, in this case, the database. In the controller layer, the methods need request parameter values. The request object is available only if the application is running in containers. In JavaEE, most of the application has many dependencies. So testing such an application becomes a headache. In such situations, the testing will be carried out with the help of dummy objects. These dummy objects are called mock objects.

Mock testing

The testing which is carried out with the help of mock objects is called mock testing. There are a number of ways which provide the means for mock testing. Let's discover them one by one.

Spring testing framework

Spring provides an API to conduct testing using the mock technique in JUnit. Using this API, we can create mock objects of `Request`, `Response`, `Filter`, and `HttpSession`, which is otherwise available from the container. All those methods which are dependent on request or user's request and response can now be tested easily without a container. Using this API, tests can be created even before the development of the controller has been completed with mocking or stubbing.

Let's use it in our controller testing which we developed in `Ch_05_jdbcTemplate_ Transaction_Declarative` as per the following cases:

Case1 – Inserting contact with correct values as per validation rules

Let's now write mock testing for the `AddController` with the help of the following steps to find out how mock objects can be initialized:

1. Create a new JUnit test case with the name `TestAddController` in the package `com.packt.ch06.controllers.test` and in this package by selecting all three methods from `AddController`.

2. Annotate it with the following:

   ```
   @WebAppConfiguration
   @ContextConfiguration({ "file:WebContent/WEB-INF/DataWeb-servlet.
   xml","classpath:connection.xml" })
   @RunWith(value = SpringJUnit4ClassRunner.class)
   ```

   JUnit has the `@RunWith` annotation, which tests by invoking the class that has been passed to it as a parameter. In our case, it is `SpringJUnit4ClassRunner`.

   `@ContextConfiguration` is used to load the configuration files which have been used to create objects using the Spring container. The location of a file can be specified by `file:` to load files from folders, or `classpath:` to load files from the `classpath`.

   `@WebApplicationContext` is used to declare that `ApplicationContext` loaded for testing is a `WebApplicationContext`.

3. Declare the data members as `MockHttpServletRequest`, `MockHttpServletResponse`, and `ModelAndView`, `AddController`.

4. Annotate the `AddController` with `@Autowired`.

5. Initialize them in the `setup` method as follows:

   ```
   @Before
     public void setUp() throws Exception {
       modelAndView = new ModelAndView();
       response = new MockHttpServletResponse();
   }
   ```

6. The data members will be set to null in `tearDown()` as follows:

   ```
   @After
     public void tearDown() throws Exception {
       modelAndView = null;
       addController = null;
       response = null;
   }
   ```

7. Let's write the code to test `addContact()` from `AddController` in `testAddContact()`. In order to carry out positive testing, we need to pass the first parameter as objects of contact. Initialize it with all correct values according to the validation rules as follows:

```
Contact contact = new Contact();
        contact.setAddress("Mumbai");
        contact.setEmail("com@packt.com");
        contact.setFirstName("t_first");
        contact.setGender(1);
        contact.setLastName("t_last");
        contact.setPhone_number("9876008990");
```

8. Initialize `BindingResult` as follows:

```
BindingResult bindingResult = new BeanPropertyBindingResult(
        contact, "contact");
```

9. Let's invoke the method `addContact()` and do the assertion. As the return type is `modelAndView`, we can find out whether the name of the view is `"manageContact"`. If it's returning a result, we can conclude it is working correctly, else there is some problem in the code. It can be done as follows:

```
modelAndView =
addController.addContact(contact,bindingResult);
        assertEquals("manageContact", modelAndView.getViewName());
```

10. The complete code snippet for `testAddContact()` will be as follows:

```
@Test
  public void testAddContact() {
    try {
      Contact contact = new Contact();
      contact.setAddress("Mumbai");
      contact.setEmail("com@packt.com");
      contact.setFirstName("t");
      contact.setGender(1);
      contact.setLastName("test_1");
      contact.setPhone_number("9876008990");

      BindingResult bindingResult = new BeanPropertyBindingResult(
          contact, "contact");

      ModelAndView modelAndView = addController.
addContact(contact,
          bindingResult);
      assertEquals("manageContact", modelAndView.getViewName());
```

```
    } catch (Exception e) {
       // TODO Auto-generated catch block
    Fail(e.getMessage());
    }


  }
```

11. On execution of the test, it will be successfully executed and checked from the output shown in the following screenshot:

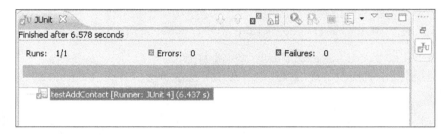

12. Also we can check in `mysql` whether one record has been inserted in the `contact_core` table.

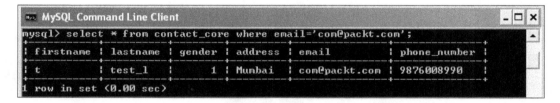

Case2 – Inserting a contact by violating validation rules for contacts

One of the reasons why the test will fail is when the `Contact` object does not contain property values as per the validation rules specified in `validation.properties` which we wrote in *Chapter 3, Working on the Presentation Layer*, for form validation. The e-mail and first name have e-mail and minimum length criteria respectively. We will violate these two rules and check what happens as shown in the following code:

```
@Test
  public void testAddContact_negative() {
    try {
      Contact contact = new Contact();
```

```
        BindingResult bindingResult = new BeanPropertyBindingResult(
            contact, "contact");
        bindingResult.reject("NotEmpty.contact.email", "default
message");
        bindingResult.reject("NotEmpty.contact.FirstName", "name must be
filled");
        modelAndView=addController.addContact(contact, bindingResult);
        assertEquals("contactForm",modelAndView.getViewName());
        assertEquals("NotEmpty.contact.email", bindingResult.
getAllErrors()
            .get(0).getCode());
        assertEquals(2,bindingResult.getAllErrors().size());

    } catch (Exception e) {
    // TODO: handle exception
    fail("test failed"+e.getMessage());

    e.printStackTrace();
    }
}
```

We are setting the rules for `BindingResult` and then cross-checking it with the help
of assertion. The above test will execute successfully and no record will get added in
the table as well.

Here we will only be able to find whether the contact object is following the
validation rules or not. If the rules are not being followed, then the validation
will fail. We created the contact object with no values to the data members. We
have bound two validation rules against which the test case has been written. The
validation triggered before the controller method gets invoked; so just by invoking
the controller and passing the binding result, we cannot prove that the validation is
being done correctly. In order to test it correctly with all rules, we need to construct
and call the URL to which our controller is mapped. But to know which field is not
following the validation rule, we need to write extra code with `HandlerMapping`,
which will make the code lengthier and complex. The solution has been provided
by the Spring testing framework with the `MockMVC` class. The `MockMVC` class does the
testing with mock requesting, annotations, and many more. `MockMVC` gives a facility
to perform requests. We can use it even when the code to test is not completely
implemented. The `MockMVC` API helps to test request mappings, type conversion,
and binding errors without the actual containers.

The following are the two ways to create an object of MockMVC:

- With loading the Spring configuration as follows:

```
@RunWith(SpringJUnit4ClassRunner.class)
@WebAppConfiguration
@ContextConfiguration("DataWeb-servlet-context.xml")
public class MyControllerTests {

@Autowired
private WebApplicationContext wac;

private MockMvc mockMvc;

@Before
public void setup() {
this.mockMvc = MockMvcBuilders.webAppContextSetup(this.wac).
build();
    }

}
```

- Without loading the Spring configuration:

```
public class MyControllerTests {

private MockMvc mockMvc;

@Before
public void setup() {
this.mockMvc = MockMvcBuilders.standaloneSetup(new
AddController()).build();
    }

}
```

Standalone setups are closer to unit testing as they test one controller at a time. Standalone setup needs to inject the dependencies with mocks manually. To create a mock object, mocking frameworks such as EasyMock and Mokito can be used. Standalone setups are more focused on finding out if any specific Spring MVC configuration is required. When the Spring configuration is loaded and used, it is integration testing and not unit testing with the help of the TesContext framework. Before going into how to implement MockMVC testing, let's have a look into MockMVC and the methods it provides for testing.

To create an object of `MockMVC`, the `MockMvcBuilders.xxx` method will be used as shown above. It has just created an object which now needs an initialization of the method to invoke from the controller. To invoke the controller method, we need to tell which method to invoke and the URL on which the method will be invoked. `MockMVCRequestBuilder` helps to build these URLs with methods as get, post, delete and many more. The code will be like the following:

```
mockMvc.perform(  MockMvcRequestBuilders  .post("/addContact.htm")
```

If the `/addContact` URL is not required to have any further initialization such as request parameters or anything else, we are set to start with testing. But sometimes, the demand of the method can be greater. In the method `addContact()` from `AddController` is expected to have `@ModelAttribute` which accepts the object of contact on form submission. To handle form submission, `contactType()` has to be used along with form parameters and their values. Once the initialization is completed, it's time to cross-check the result. The `addExpect()` method helps us to test the results with `MockMvcResultMatchers`. `MockMvcResultMatchers` has methods such as `view()`, `mode()`, `json()`, `content()`, and `cookies()` for helping us in testing. We will use these practically in the upcoming examples to carry out mock testing.

We have done a lot on unit testing. Now let's discover the integration testing with `MockMVC` in Spring.

Why integration testing?

In real-world software development, each application development is divided into a number of small modules. These modules will be developed by different developers. It's very important to find out how such separately developed modules when combined together are working. Each application is developed in different layers, such as UI, business layer, and DAO layer. In each layer, the data which is accepted, processed, and passed may be in a different format. So it's very important to find out whether the data passed and collected is correct or not, otherwise there will be a manipulation problem. Integration testing is also important as developers face a big problem in meeting continuous changes in requirement. Integration testing helps to find out problems of collaboration on layers at an early stage instead of getting it in later stages of development.

Let's implement this in our application to test form validation:

1. Create a new `JunitTest` case `TestAddController_standAlone` in the `com.packt.ch06.controllers.test` package.

2. Declare `MockMVC` and `AddController` as data members.

3. As `Addcontroller` has its own dependencies and we will not use any frameworks to create `Mock` objects, we simply use `@Autowired` on `AddController` for DI.

4. Override `setup()` to initialize `MockMVC` as follows:

```
@Before
  public void setUp() throws Exception {

    mockMvc=MockMvcBuilders
        .standaloneSetup(addController).build();

  }
```

5. Let's test `addContact()` from the `AddController` in `testAddContact_ positive`. In order to test this method, we need to set up `perform()` as:

   ◦ URL to `/addContact` for `post` method.

   ◦ Content type to application form `urlencoded`.

   ◦ All the request parameters as specified in `contactForm.jsp` in order to initialize a contact object according to the validation rules specified in `validation.properties`.

   ◦ The method `addContact()` has `@ModelAttribute` as a parameter which specifies there is an attribute with the name `contact`. So while carrying out testing, we need to set the same attribute for the `request` object.

6. The testing will be done for the result with `andExpect()` which will be for :

   ◦ The result view as `manageContact`.

   ◦ The attribute ID with the value specified at the time of contact initialization.

   ◦ In the `addContact()` from `AddController`, we set the attribute `id` to value email from contact object. In the code above, we set the `email` parameter for value `packt@test.com`, so we will consider the same value while testing.

7. We will use `MockMvcResultHandlers.print()` which helps to print values. The code will be as follows:

```
@Test
  public void testAddContact() {

    try {
```

```
         mockMvc.perform(
            MockMvcRequestBuilders
               .post("/addContact.htm")
               .contentType(                    MediaType.
APPLICATION_FORM_URLENCODED)
               .param("email", "packt@test.com")
               .param("firstName", "first_n")
               .param("lastName", "last_n")
               .param("address", "testing address")
               .param("phone_number", "9191919191")
               .param("gender", "1")
               .requestAttr("contact", new Contact()))

         .andExpect(
         MockMvcResultMatchers.view().name("manageContact"))
         .andExpect(
            MockMvcResultMatchers.model().attribute("id",
               "packt@test.com"));
   } catch (Exception e) {
     // TODO: handle exception
     fail(e.getMessage());
   }
  }
```

8. On executing, the test will pass and on the console, we will get output as follows:

```
MockHttpServletRequest:
        HTTP Method = POST
        Request URI = /addContact.htm
        Parameters = {email=[packt@test.com],
firstName=[first_n],
lastName=[last_n],
address=[testing address],
phone_number=[9191919191],
gender=[1]}
        Headers = {Content-Type=[application/x-www-form-
urlencoded]}

        Handler:
               Type = com.packt.ch06.controllers.AddController
      Method = public
```

```
org.springframework.web.servlet.ModelAndViewcom.packt.ch06.
controllers.AddController.addContact(com.packt.ch06.pojo.
Contact,org.springframework.validation.BindingResult) throws java.
lang.Exception
   Resolved Exception:
               Type = null
ModelAndView:
           View name = manageContact
           View = null
           Attribute = genderList
           value =
           [com.packt.ch06.pojo.Gender@17ebe66,
            com.packt.ch06.pojo.Gender@6279d]
           Attribute = contact
           value =
               com.packt.ch06.pojo.Contact@1b11b
            errors = []
            Attribute = id
            value = packt@test.com

FlashMap:

MockHttpServletResponse:
               Status = 200
Error message = null
               Headers = {}
        Content type = null
               Body =
        Forwarded URL = manageContact
   Redirected URL = null
           Cookies = []
```

The preceding code was of positive form validation testing to add a contact. Now we will do negative testing where we submit a form with violations of some validation rules. We will not follow the validation rules for e-mail and first name and will carry out testing. Setting parameters will be the same process but to check the result we will consider:

- The view is contactForm
- There are errors in the fields set for the form
- Email and first name are not set as per validation rules

Let's develop `testAddContact_negative()` in `TestAddController_negative` to find what is output when a form with validation errors is submitted. The code will be as follows:

```
@Test
public void testAddContact_negative() {
  try {

    mockMvc.perform(
        MockMvcRequestBuilders.post("/addContact.htm")
.contentType(MediaType.APPLICATION_FORM_URLENCODED)
        .param("email", "packt").param("firstName", "f")
.param("lastName", "last_n")
        .param("address", "testing address")
        .param("phone_number", "9191919191")
        .param("gender", "1")
        .requestAttr("contact", new Contact()))    .andExpect(MockMv
cResultMatchers.view().name("contactForm"))
        .andExpect(
            MockMvcResultMatchers
              .model()
              .attributeHasFieldErrors("contact", "email"))   .andE
xpect(MockMvcResultMatchers.model()
              .attributeHasFieldErrors("contact",
                  "firstName"))
        .andDo(MockMvcResultHandlers.print());

  } catch (Exception e) {
    // TODO: handle exception
    fail(e.getMessage());
  }
}
```

The method `model().attributeHasFiledErrors` accepts the attribute name and the field where the validation error is. We had set `@ModelAttribute 'contact'` which has `email` and `firstname` as data members with validation errors. We will check this with code as follows:

```
model().attributeHasFieldErrors("contact", "email"))
model().attributeHasFieldErrors("contact",  "firstName"))
```

On executing, the result output on the console is as follows:

```
MockHttpServletRequest:
        HTTP Method = POST
        Request URI = /addContact.htm
        Parameters = {email=[packt],
firstName=[f],
lastName=[last_n],
address=[testing address],
phone_number=[9191919191], gender=[1]}
        Headers = {Content-Type=[application/x-www-form-urlencoded]}

Handler:
        Type = com.packt.ch06.controllers.AddController
        Method = public org.springframework.web.servlet.ModelAndView
            com.packt.ch06.controllers.AddController.addContact
            (com.packt.ch06.pojo.Contact,org.springframework.
            validation.BindingResult) throws java.lang.Exception

Resolved Exception:
            Type = null

ModelAndView:
        View name = contactForm
        View = null
        Attribute = genderList
value = [com.packt.ch06.pojo.Gender@a45a24,
                    com.packt.ch06.pojo.Gender@1a1ff9]
        Attribute = contact
value = com.packt.ch06.pojo.Contact@c789fb
errors = [Field error in object 'contact' on field 'email':
rejected value [packt]; codes
                [Email.contact.email,Email.email,Email.java.
lang.String,Email]; arguments
[org.springframework.context.support.
DefaultMessageSourceResolvable: codes
                [contact.email,email]; arguments []; default message
[email],
[Ljavax.validation.constraints.Pattern$Flag;@12943ac, [A-
Za-z0-9._%+-]+@[A-Za-z0-9.-]+\.[A-Za-z]{2,4}]; default message [not a
well-formed email address],
Field error in object 'contact' on field 'firstName':
rejected value [f]; codes
[Length.contact.firstName,
Length.firstName,Length.java.lang.String,Length];
```

```
                   Arguments
[org.springframework.context.support.
DefaultMessageSourceResolvable: codes
[contact.firstName,firstName]; arguments [];


default message [firstName],10,2]; default message
[length must be between 2 and 10]]


FlashMap:


MockHttpServletResponse:
             Status = 200
      Error message = null
            Headers = {}
       Content type = null
               Body =
      Forwarded URL = contactForm
     Redirected URL = null
            Cookies = []
```

If we observe the `errors` field from `modelandview` it shows two reject values. It also shows a message which we set in the `validation.properties` file for `email` and `firstName` fields as:

```
[A-Za-z0-9._%+-]+@[A-Za-z0-9.-]+\.[A-Za-z]{2,4}]; default message [not
a well-formed email address],
default message [firstName],10,2]; default message
                      [length must be between 2 and 10]]
```

Also the view name is shown as:

```
        Forwarded URL = contactForm
```

Let's test `showContactForm()`. This method accepts `request`, `response`, and `map` objects. We need to do the following:

- Set request object for `'/showContact'` URI
- Create an object of `ExtendedMap` as `mock` object and add to it the object of `contact`

The code to carry out the test in `testShowForm( )` will be as follows:

```
@Test
  public void testShowContactForm() {
    try {
```

```
Contact contact = new Contact();
ExtendedModelMap map=new ExtendedModelMap();
map.addAttribute(contact);
mockMvc.perform(MockMvcRequestBuilders.post("/addContact.htm"))
    .andExpect(MockMvcResultMatchers.status().isOk())
    .andExpect(MockMvcResultMatchers.view().name("contactForm"))
    .andExpect(
        MockMvcResultMatchers.model().attributeExists(
        "contact")).andDo(MockMvcResultHandlers.print());
} catch (Exception e) {
// TODO Auto-generated catch block
fail(e.getMessage());
}


}
```

On execution of the test, it will print the following trace on the console:

```
MockHttpServletRequest:
        HTTP Method = POST
        Request URI = /showForm.htm
         Parameters = {}
            Headers = {}


Handler:
               Type = com.packt.ch06.controllers.AddController
             Method = public org.springframework.web.
servlet.ModelAndViewcom.packt.ch06.controllers.AddController.
showContactForm(javax.servlet.http.HttpServletRequest,javax.servlet.
http.HttpServletResponse,org.springframework.ui.ModelMap) throws java.
lang.Exception


Resolved Exception:
               Type = null


ModelAndView:
          View name = contactForm
                          View = null
          Attribute = genderList
              value = [com.packt.ch06.pojo.Gender@6d3b92,
                       com.packt.ch06.pojo.Gender@162198b]
          Attribute = contact value = com.packt.ch06.pojo.
          Contact@17b1d64errors = []
```

```
FlashMap:

MockHttpServletResponse:
             Status = 200
      Error message = null
            Headers = {}
       Content type = null
               Body =
      Forwarded URL = /WEB-INF/jsps/contactForm.jsp
     Redirected URL = null
            Cookies = []
```

It's clear from the trace that an object of Contact got added to the contactForm URI. Here we used the technique of MockMVC where we are using the actual implementation of the controllers but frameworks such as EasyMock, Mockito, and Arquillian provided the API to create mock objects.

Mockito testing

Mockito is an open source framework used in conjunction with JUnit for testing. Mockito helps in creating Mock objects to be used while testing. Mockito tests help in reducing the tight coupling by removing the requirement of the expectation specification. Mockito creates mock objects with the static method mock() provided by the org.mockito.Mockito class. In Mockito, the when() method defines the action to be taken and then Return() returns the result of the action. When() can define a method call and thenReturn() is expected to return from the method. The when() accepts the argument of the method to be invoked and the result to be returned will be the argument of thenReturn(). when() accepts the method under testing and thenReturn() returns the result which we use for assertion. Methods such as anyString(), anyInt() are used to define independent values from the methods. Mockito can be used for behavioral testing as well. In behavior testing, a certain result is expected on invocation of the method with some values. Mockito provides verify() to find out whether the method is called with some typical values or not. But we cannot use Mockito to test final class, anonymous classes, and primitive types.

Let's develop one sample Mockito test for ContactBussinessImpl in our application using the following steps:

1. Create a new JUnit test case with the name TestContactBussiness in com.packt.ch06.controllers.test.

2. Select addContact(), findContact(), and findAllContacts() methods for testing.

3. Declare `ContactBussinessImpl`, and `ContactDAOImpl`. These two data members have to be mocked in order to get object and invoke methods on it. The class `ContactBussinessImpl` has a dependency `ContactDAOImpl`. The class under testing `ContactBussinessImpl` is annotated as `@InjectMocks` and its dependency `ContactDAOImpl` to inject has to be annotated as `@Mock`. The code will be as follows:

```
@InjectMocks
  ContactBussinessImpl bussinessImpl;
@Mock
  ContactDAOImpl contactDAOImpl;
```

4. Initialize Mockito in `setup()` as:

```
@Before
  public void setUp() throws Exception {
    MockitoAnnotations.initMocks(this);
  }
```

5. Add `testAddContact()` to test `addContact()` from `ContactBussinessImpl`:

   ° In `testAddContact()`, we first have to create a contact and using `when()` we invoke the method on the mock object of contact and will return the expected value from `thenReturn()`. We will assume here that the returned value is `1`. This is our expected value.

   ° Now invocation of the actual business logic method will give the actual value.

   ° Using `assert`, we will cross-check expected and actual values to test the result. The code will be as follows:

```
@Test
  public void testAddContact() {
    Contact contact = new Contact();
    contact.setAddress("address1");
    contact.setEmail("test2@test.com");
    contact.setFirstName("first");
    contact.setLastName("last");
    contact.setGender(1);
    contact.setPhone_number("1212121212");
    Mockito.when(
contactDAOImpl.addContact(contact)).thenReturn(1);

    int result=bussinessImpl.addContact(contact);
    assertEquals(1,result);
  }
```

6. The above test will execute successfully. In the same way, we can test `FindContact` as follows:

```
@Test
  public void testFindContact() {
    Contact contact = new Contact();
    contact.setAddress("address1");
    contact.setEmail("test2@test.com");
    contact.setFirstName("first");
    contact.setLastName("last");
    contact.setGender(1);
    contact.setPhone_number("1212121212");
    Mockito.when(contactDAOImpl.findContact("test2@test.com")).
thenReturn(contact);

    Contact contact2=bussinessImpl.findContact("test2@test.com");
    assertEquals("test2@test.com", contact2.getEmail());
  }
```

7. The test case for `findAllContacts` will be as follows:

```
@Test
  public void testFindAllContcats() {
    List<Contact>contacts=new ArrayList<Contact>();
    Contact contact = new Contact();
    contact.setAddress("address1");
    contact.setEmail("test2@test.com");
    contact.setFirstName("first");
    contact.setLastName("last");
    contact.setGender(1);
    contact.setPhone_number("1212121212");
    contacts.add(contact);
    contacts.add(contact);
    Mockito.when(contactDAOImpl.findAllContcats()).
thenReturn(contacts);
    List<Contact> contacts2=bussinessImpl.findAllContcats();

    assertEquals(contacts.size(),contacts2.size());
  }
```

In the preceding code, we discussed testing the business layer. The controller layer can also be tested on the same line but the way of writing the code will be bit different. Let's develop a test case for addContact() with the help of the following steps:

1. Create a new JUnit test case with the name TestAddController_Mokito in the test package for addContact() for testing.

2. Declare AddController and ContactBussinessImpl and BeanPropertyBindingResult as data members. The AddController has dependency of ContactBussinessImpl. Both of these classes need to be mocked to fulfill the dependency with the creation of objects. The code will be as follows:

```
@InjectMocks
  AddController addController;
@Mock
  ContactBussinessImpl bussinessImpl;
@Mock
  BeanPropertyBindingResult bindingResult;
```

3. Initialize the Mockito in setup() as follows:

```
@Before
  public void setUp() throws Exception {
    MockitoAnnotations.initMocks(this);
  }
```

4. Declare testAddContact() where we write the test code:

    °   With the help of when()-thenReturn(), we will return an expected value on execution of bussinessImpl.addContact().

    °   With the actual invocation of the controller's addContact method, we will get an object of ModelAndView, using which we will extract value from the modelMap.

    °   We will assert the size of the entries and the attribute value from map as well.

The code will be as follows:

```
@Test
  public void testAddContact()
  {
    Contact contact = new Contact();
    contact.setAddress("address1");
```

```
contact.setEmail("abc@abc.com");
contact.setFirstName("first");
contact.setLastName("last");
contact.setGender(1);
contact.setPhone_number("1212121212");
when(bussinessImpl.addContact(contact)).thenReturn(1);

try {
  ModelAndView modelAndView =
          addController.addContact(contact, bindingResult);
  Set<Map.Entry<String,Object>> entries =
          modelAndView.getModel().entrySet();
  Iterator iterator=entries.iterator();
    String val=null;
  while (iterator.hasNext()) {
    Map.Entry entry=(Map.Entry)iterator.next();
    val=(String)entry.getValue();
  }
  assertEquals(1,entries.size());
  assertEquals("abc@abc.com",val);

} catch (Exception e) {
  // TODO Auto-generated catch block
  fail(e.getMessage());
}
}
```

In the same way, we can carry out the testing for getContact(). The snippet code to carry out testing will be as follows:

```
@Test
public void testGetContact()
{
  Contact contact = new Contact();
  contact.setAddress("address1");
  contact.setEmail("abc@abc.com");
  contact.setFirstName("first");
  contact.setLastName("last");
  contact.setGender(1);
  contact.setPhone_number("1212121212");
  when(bussinessImpl.findContact("abc@abc.com")).
thenReturn(contact);
```

```
    ModelAndViewmodelAndView=searchAnnotController.getContcat("abc@
abc.com");
    Set<Map.Entry<String,Object>> entries =
            modelAndView.getModel().entrySet();
    Iterator iterator=entries.iterator();
    Contact contact2=null;
    while (iterator.hasNext()) {
      Map.Entry entry=(Map.Entry)iterator.next();
      contact2=(Contact)entry.getValue();
    }
    assertEquals(contact.getEmail(),contact2.getEmail());
  }
```

The preceding code execution shows that we are testing the controllers and business logic code without loading any configuration files from the Spring controller and also no container is required. In the same way, a new framework, Arquillian, has been introduced to carry out testing without bothering about the dependencies of the application.

Arquillian

Arquillian is the latest tool developed by Jboss.org which provides a satisfactory solution to writing functional and integration tests. Arquillian provides a facility to execute the test in the server environment, which can take advantage of using the resources provided by the containers. Arquillian supports integration with containers such as Tomcat, Glassfish, and JBoss. It has ShrinkWrap, which provides modules for creating archives, descriptors, and resolvers. It also supports running the tests in the cloud and has remote and embedded containers:

- The remote container resides on a separate JVM from the test runner.
- The embedded container resides in the same JVM in the same test runner.

Arquillian comprises a unit testing framework, ShrinkWrap, and target containers. Arquillian bundles the test cases, dependent classes and resources in an archive. It deploys the archives in a container that supports Arquillian tests and the result will be reported to the test runner.

Summary

Application development is a lengthy and time-consuming process. In each step, there are multiple loopholes where there is a chance of making mistakes. All such mistakes will club together to make a blunder. If this got caught at the end when the final product testing is carried out, it's of no use and the developers will run short of time for development. In this chapter, we discussed various steps such as unit testing, integration testing, and the modules to use for application development in order to reduce the errors in the development with testing. We also saw the complexities to manage request and response objects for carrying out unit testing of controllers. The example covered here showed the use of mock objects. We saw various ways, such as the Spring framework and Mockito, to create such Mock objects. We also covered the `MockMVC` object to carry out integration testing.

Now we have a working product, but we haven't taken any measures for securing URLs such as `addContact` and restricted them to be used by the authorized users only. In the next chapter, we will cover the security techniques to be applied to authenticate the authorized users and give them access to use the URLs.

Securing the Application

7

We have developed an application where we are maintaining contacts. This information is right now publicly available. Anybody can come, visit my page, click on the link and get the contact details. Anybody can even add contacts. What is the assurance that the data which is being added is correct and not false? That the person who is entering the data is genuine? No! It's not at all guaranteed, which leads to a serious problem of data protection. We need to protect the application data so that it is not mishandled and all possible care has to be taken from the developers' side to make sure that the reliability of data will remain intact. In this chapter, we are going to learn and explore how security helps to protect the data from getting used by an unknown user. In this chapter, we will cover:

- What is security and why do we need it?
- How to secure web applications using Spring
- Application layer security
- Custom security

Make it safe, make it secure

On the Web, all data gets transferred through a channel where it is possible for someone else to steal the information which you are sending or receiving from the server. This stolen data can be misused and can affect the website as well as the user badly. Let's take the example of accessing mail accounts. Whenever we try to access our mail accounts, the URL gets changed from HTTP to HTTPS, which shows we are going to access something secure. Some extra measures have been taken in order to protect the data as it goes to and fro, from the security perspective.

The security consists of the following:

- **Authentication**: This is the process by which the application checks whether the user is who they are claiming to be or not. If we want to check our e-mails, we cannot do it directly unless and until we prove that we are the right person. How do we do that? For that, we need to provide our mail ID and correct password. The application will check if this e-mail ID and password pair is correct or not, and take the steps accordingly. Sometimes, it may be possible that someone hacks your password and accesses the account. The system cannot do physical checking. The one who provides correct authentication information will get the data.

- **Authorization**: On the Web, there are some specific URLs which can be accessed by some specific users and these links will not be available to the rest of the users. These are role-based links which can be accessed only if you have a respective role to perform a specific action. This is termed authorization. Once a user gets authenticated, then the container checks for the role of that user in the security table. If the URL with the specified username-password pair has the correct security role, the container gives access to that page. Let's take the example of blogs. When we search Spring framework blogs, we get many links. We can visit and read them. Can we delete or update the blog? No, because the data doesn't belong to us. The addition or updating can be made only if you have an author role, otherwise not.

- **Confidentiality**: This is an arrangement which makes it difficult to steal authentication information through a channel. It can be done by encryption algorithms. Confidentiality makes sure to secure confidential information about the user, which otherwise can be seen and can be used by fake users.

- **Data integrity**: The data which we fetched from the server can be seen or altered by a middle unknown resource. Data integrity ensures the accuracy and consistency of the data throughout the application.

The steps to provide security in a Web application are as follows:

1. Create a security realm. A realm is a place where the authorization information is stored.

2. In the realm, we store roles, username and password by assigning them some role.

3. Configure security constraints to specify which methods from which URL are going to be accessed by whom.

4. Provide an authentication mechanism. BASIC, FORM-BASE, CLIENTCERT, and DIGEST are the four ways which can be used for the authentication process:

    ° BASIC: The login information will be transmitted in encoded form, leading to weak security

    ° FORM: Using FORM, developers can design their own forms through HTML

    ° DIGEST: Transmits login information in a more secure way but the encryption mechanism used is not in wide use

    ° CLIENTCERT: This is the most secure form to transmit the information using a key

5. Provide configuration for the transport guarantee as CONFIDENTIAL to give data integrity/confidentiality.

Spring security framework

Spring provides a handy, well-defined, declarative solution to provide security by handling authentication and authorization at both request level and method invocation level. Spring provides two ways to handle security:

- Servlet filters: To handle Web request and URL access restrictions
- Spring AOP: To handle secure method invocations

Spring provides eight modules to handle Spring Security, as follows:

Module	Description
ACL	This provides support for domain object security via access control lists. The `org.springframework.security.acls` package enables developers to use it.
CAS Client	This provides integration with JA-SIG's Central Authentication Service. The `org.springframework.security.cas` package enables developers to use it.
Configuration	This contains support for Spring Security's XML namespace. The `org.springframework.security.config` package enables developers to use it.

Module	Description
Core	This provides the Spring Security library, which supports standalone applications, service layer, JDBC user provisioning and remote clients.
LDAP	This provides support for authentication using Lightweight Directory Access. The `org.springframework.security.ldap` package enables developers to use it.
OpenID	This provides integration with the OpenID standard. The `org.springframework.security.openid` package enables developers to use it.
Web	This provides filter-based web Spring Security support. The `org.springframework.security.web` package enables developers to use it.
Tag Library	Includes a set of JSP tags to provide security

It's not necessary to add all these eight modules in your web application; it all depends on what facilities you want and how you want to provide security.

As we have a web application, we need web, core, and configuration modules. If we decide to go for handling security in JSP, then the Tag Library module needs to be added. These modules will be provided by `Spring security-core.jar`, `Spring-security-config.jar`, and `Spring-security-web.jar`.

Secure web request

Everything in the Web is going to be accessed through a URL which is handled by requests. The process of securing web applications starts from making secure requests. In the application, find all those URLs which need to be handled with some authority. The content of these URLs will be available only if the user is authorized. Sometimes, we also need to provide data security through HTTPS, providing **Secure Service Layer (SSL)**. Whenever a user wants to access the data from the secure URL, he or she needs to provide authentication credentials so that the application will be able to recognize the user. If the user has the correct authentication and has the right privilege, then the data will be given to the user, otherwise not.

Way 1 – Spring Security for URL using servlet filters

The following diagram illustrates the working of Spring Security using servlet filters:

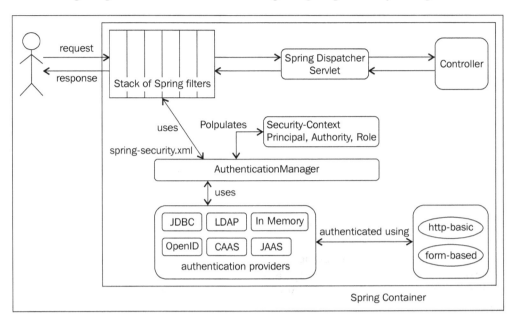

The process can be described as follows:

- When a request for a resource is raised, it will be first compared to the URL mapped in web.xml for <filter-mapping>. If a match is found, the request is delegated to the bean having the ID springSecurityFilterChain.

- This 'springSecurityFilterChain' bean returns an instance of the filterChainProxy bean, which consists of a list of security filters defined in the Spring context to invoke, which provides security. The initialization of filterChainProxy and its registration in a Spring context takes place when HttpSecurityBeanDefinationParser reads <http> using spring the security namespace.

- Let's take the filterChainProxy initialization a bit further. Let us assume we have written a very basic configuration of <http> as:

```
<http>
  <form-login>
  <http-basic>
<logout>
```

The `<http>` sets up the `FilterChainProxy` which is delegated to `DelegatingFilterProxy` which has been configured in the `web.xml`. The default `<http>` block creates `SecurityContextPersistenceFilter`, `ExceptionTransalationFilter` and `filterSecurityInterceptor`. The above configuration adds three more filters as `BasicAuthenticationFilter`, `LogoutFilter`, and `UsernamePasswordAuthenticationFilter` in the filter chain. So, by default, `filterChainProxy` initializes a series of filters to be invoked. It can also be possible to choose the filters to be invoked in `filterChain` by defining our own configuration as:

```
<bean id="filterChainProxy" class="org.springframework.security.web.
FilterChainProxy">
<filter-chain-map path="abc">
<filter-chain pattern="/contact" filters="none"/>
<filter-chain pattern="/addContact.htm"
filters="logoutFilter,formLoginFilter,
exceptionTranslator, filterSecurityInterceptor"/>
<filter-chain-map>
</bean>
```

We configure `DelegatingFilterProxy` in `web.xml`, which delegates to the filter implementation that has been defined in the spring application context as a bean by taking advantage of Spring Dependency Injection. When Spring loads the configuration file, and if it gets `<http auto-config="true" >` configuration, it sets up the security. It will be done by registering the filter stack, protected URLs, and `FilterChainProxy` with the name `'springSecurityFilterChain'`. So the name of this filter is used to look up the filter bean, which has the same ID in the configuration file. Alternatively, we can do the configuration in another way, as follows:

```
<bean  id="springSecurityFilterChain" class="org.springframework.
security.web.FilterChainProxy">
```

Spring provides many filters which can be used for Spring Security, which got woven by the filter chain. Let's have a look at some of the filters:

- `LogoutFilter`: This filter checks that if the request is for `/j_spring_security_logout` to provide a default logout handler. If it is not a logout request, it will be passed on to the next filter.

- `BasicAuthenticationFilter`: This filter attempts the process of basic login authentication, if a header for basic authentication is found in the request.

- `DefaultLoginPageGeneratingFilter`: If the request for `/spring_security_login` is received, then it will return a default login form, otherwise the request will pass on to the next filter.

- `UsernamePasswordAuthenticationFilter`: This filter checks for the request with URL /j_spring_security_check to read values of j_username and j_password to perform authentication using `AuthenticationManager`.

If we are using the default configuration, then the Spring framework loads the following:

- The authentication manager to be used, which defines all the authentication providers available for the application.

- The authentication provider has implementation of `UserDetailsService`. Spring loads the user login information in this `UserDetailsService` to perform the comparison of authentication credentials.

The authentication information can be stored in one of the two ways, as described:

- In an application context: The login information, along with user role, can be configured in the XML file as:

```
<authentication-manager id="authenticationmanager">
<authentication-provider>
<user-service>
<user name="admin" password="admin" authorities="ROLE_USER"/>
<user name="guest" password="guest" authorities="ROLE_USER"/>
</user-service>
</authentication-provider>
</authentication-manager>
```

- In the database: If we want to check the login data against the database, we need to provide the following configuration:

```
<authentication-manager id="authenticationmanager">
<authentication-provider>
<jdbc-user-service data-source-ref="dataSource">
</jdbc-user-service>
</authentication-provider>
</authentication-manager>
```

The dataSource is another bean which is used to obtain the connection, as discussed in the Spring-JDBC integration section:

- The `<http>` configuration is checked to provide the authentication mechanism. The authentication mechanism includes rendering of the login page as follows:

  ° It checks the configuration for whether it is basic authentication or form-based authentication. Depending upon the information, a login page will be provided to the user where the credentials can be entered.

- ° If we are using basic authentication, the login credentials are sent to the server under the authentication `http` header. This now will be further handled by `BasicAuthenticationFilter`.

- ° If we are using form-based authentication, the login credentials are checked against data provided by the spring context to authenticate the user.

If the user gets authenticated with the help of the authentication mechanism, then it's time to check the authorization:

- The filter does the authentication for the roles and credential with the help of `AuthenticationSuccessHandler`. If all the information matches, the handler takes the user to the success page, otherwise `AuthenticationFailureHandler` redirects the request to the authentication page or the failure page respectively.

Let's use the following flow chart to understand security mechanism in an easy way:

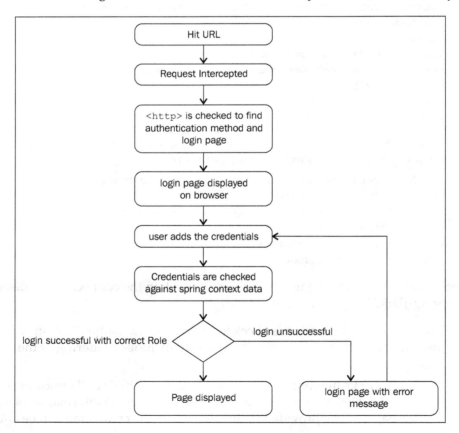

The process flow is as described here:

1. The user hits the URL to visit.

2. Hitting the URL, we make a request to the application. In order to find out which resource is mapped to the URL, DD will be hit. The filter mapping will be checked to find out if the resource is having limited access. If it is secure, `<http>` configuration will be observed. The `<http>` configuration is checked for the authentication mechanism to discover which authentication method to be used, login form location, and other required information.

3. If its `<http-basic>`, a default login page by spring is provided where the user can enter his credentials. If form-based authentication is configured, a custom login form will be given.

4. The data will be taken to the server for authentication.

5. `<authentication-manager>` is checked to find how to load the credential data.

6. Authentication is performed and, depending upon it, a success or failure page will be shown to the user.

Let's start securing the URL for adding the contact data in our contact management. The URL which we want to make secure is showForm.htm. Only ROLE_ADMIN can access the URL to get the contact form and to add new contact; other roles cannot access the information. Let's take Ch04_JdbcTemplate_Integraion to add Spring Security with basic authentication with the help of the following steps.

Case 1 – Basic authentication

Perform the following steps for basic authentication:

1. Create a new XML named spring-security.xml in WEB-INF.

2. Add a new namespace to capture common uses of the framework and simplify the syntax in the XML configuration file as xmlns:security=http://www.springframework.org/schema/security which is mapped to the schema locations such as:

   http://www.springframework.org/schema/securityhttp://www.springframework.org/schema/security/spring-security-3.0.xsd

The XML will look like this:

```
<?xml version="1.0" encoding="UTF-8"?>
<beans xmlns="http://www.springframework.org/schema/beans"
  xmlns:security="http://www.springframework.org/schema/security"
  xmlns:xsi="http://www.w3.org/2001/XMLSchema-instance"
  xsi:schemaLocation="http://www.springframework.org/schema/beans
  http://www.springframework.org/schema/beans/spring-beans-3.0.xsd
  http://www.springframework.org/schema/security
 http://www.springframework.org/schema/security/spring-security-
3.2.xsd">
```

Now we can use security as the namespace to use the security tags.

1. Configure the URL, the role which can access the URL, and the
    authentication mechanism as:

    ```
    <security:http auto-config="true">
      <security:intercept-url pattern="/showForm.htm" access="ROLE_
    ADMIN"/>
      <security:http-basic/>
    </security:http>
    ```

2. Next, configure the authentication manager and authentication provider. To
    configure the authentication provider, we need to configure the user service.
    The user service configures the username, password, and role. Only the
    credential pair having the role ROLE_ADMIN can access showForm.htm. Take
    care while configuring the role which can access the URL to be prefixed with
    ROLE_. The configuration will be as follows:

    ```
    <security:authentication-manager>
        <security:authentication-provider>
          <security:user-service>
            <security:username="admin" password="admin"
              authorities="ROLE_ADMIN"/>
            <security:username="user" password="user"
              authorities="ROLE_USER" />
          </security:user-service>
        </security:authentication-provider>
      </security:authentication-manager>
    ```

    The preceding configuration defines two users: admin and user.

Configure the basic authentication mechanism under `<http>` with
`<security:http-basic>`; the complete `<http>` configuration will
be as follows:

```
<security:http auto-config="true">
    <security:intercept-url pattern="/showForm.htm" access="ROLE_
ADMIN"/>
    <security:http-basic/>
  </security:http>
```

3. Configure a filter in the `web.xml` file as follows:

```
<filter>
<filter-name>springSecurityFilterChain</filter-name>
<filter-class>
org.springframework.web.filter.DelegatingFilterProxy
</filter-class>
</filter>
```

4. As we have added a new `.xml file`, the servlet `init` param also needs to be
changed to load a new XML as follows:

```
<servlet>
<servlet-name>DataWeb</servlet-name>
<servlet-class>
org.springframework.web.servlet.DispatcherServlet
</servlet-class>
<init-param>
<param-name>contextConfigLocation</param-name>
<param-value>classpath:connection.xml WEB-INF/DataWeb-servlet.xml
WEB-INF/spring-security.xml</param-value>
</init-param>
<load-on-startup>1</load-on-startup>
</servlet>
```

5. Also configure the `ContextLoaderListener` to load all XML to register
beans in a spring context as follows:

```
<context-param>
<param-name>contextConfigLocation</param-name>
<param-value>classpath:connection.xml WEB-INF/DataWeb-servlet.xml
WEB-INF/spring-security.xml</param-value>
</context-param>
<listener>
<listener-class>org.springframework.web.context.
ContextLoaderListener</listener-class>
</listener>
```

The following are the steps to execute the application:

1. Deploy the application.

2. From the home screen, click on the **Add new Record** link. As we haven't implemented security, we are getting the Add New Contact form. However, now we will be prompted to log in. It will be as shown in the following screenshot:

3. Let's enter the credentials of a user who has 'user' as username and the password is 'user'.

4. We will get the same login form again as the user doesn't have authorization to get the form.

5. Now enter admin and admin as username and password respectively. As the credentials are matching to the role as ROLE_ADMIN, we will get the contact form to add a new contact.

Case 2 – Login form authentication

In the preceding application, we have used the login from Windows, but sometimes a customized login form will be the requirement of a project. Let's rewrite some part of the code which allows us to use a customized login form. In order to incorporate the new configuration, we just need to change a few configurations as follows:

1. Change the `<http>` configuration to support form login authentication as follows:

```
<security:http auto-config="true">
    <security:intercept-url pattern="/showForm.htm"
      access="ROLE_ADMIN"/>
    <security:form-login login-processing-url="/j_spring_security_
check"
        login-page="/login.jsp" default-target-url="/index.jsp"
        authentication-failure-url="/login.jsp?error=error"/>
```

The `<security:form-login>` takes the following attributes :

   ° **URL**: This has a value `/j_spring_security_check` that acts as the action in the form which the user is going to submit.

   ° **Login-page**: This is `/login.jsp` where the user enters the credentials.

   ° **Default url**: This will be `/index.jsp`.

   ° **Authentication-failure-url**: It has `/login.jsp?error=error`, a URL where the user is redirected if the authentication fails and the message to be shown to the user will be fetched from the request parameter error.

2. Create a `login.jsp` page to take user credentials. The values of the `action`, `name`, and `password` attributes are fixed so as to trigger the security mechanism. Display the message to the user using an error parameter. The code will look like this:

```
<html>
<body>
<jsp:include page="/WEB-INF/jsps/header.jsp"></jsp:include>
<c:set var="er"value="${param.error }"></c:set>
  <c:if test="${ er.equals('error')}">
    <c:out value="please provide correct credentials"></c:out>
  </c:if>

  <c:if test="${ not empty msg }">
    <c:out value="${msg}"></c:out>
  </c:if>
```

```
<center><br><br><br><br><br>
<b>L O G I N</b>
<br><br>

  <form action="<c:url value='/j_spring_security_
check'/>"method="post">
    <table>
      <tr style="height:50px">
        <td align="left">User Name</td>
        <td><input type="text"name="j_username"value=""></td>
      </tr>
      <tr>
        <td align="left">Password</td>
        <td><input type="password"name="j_password"></td>
      </tr>
      <tr>
        <td></td>
        <td align="right">
        <input type="submit"name="username"value="LOGIN"></td>
      </tr>

    </table>
  </form>
  </center>
</body>
</html>
```

3. Deploy the application. On clicking **Add New Record**, we will get the login.jsp page instead of getting the old window as follows:

4. If we add the credentials as admin for both username and password, we will get the contact form.

5. If we enter credentials of the user as user - user, we will get the same login page with an error message as shown in the following screenshot:

Case 3 – Authentication against database

In cases 1 and 2, we authenticated the user against the data which is configured in the authentication provider. Instead of configuring in the XML, we can store the credentials in the database and use it for authentication. To use database authentication, we need to follow the following steps:

1. In authentication-provider, instead of configuring a user service, we need to configure the jdbc-user-service as:

```
<security:authentication-manager>
    <security:authentication-provider>
      <security:jdbc-user-serviceid="userService"
        data-source-ref="dataSource"
        users-by-username-query="select username,password, enabled
from contact_users where username=?"
        authorities-by-username-query="select username, role from
contact_users where username=?"/>
    </security:authentication-provider>
```

   ° The dataSource bean will provide the details to obtain the connection

   ° The users-by-username-query queries the database for a user's username, password, and enabled status, given the username

   ° The authorities-by-username-query queries the database for a user's authorities given the username

2. Create the table `contact_users` and add a few users as follows:

```
create table contact_users(username varchar(20), password
varchar(20), role varchar(10), enabled boolean);
insert into contact_users values('admin','admin','ROLE_
ADMIN',true);
insert into contact_users values('admin1','admin','ROLE_
ADMIN',true);
insert into contact_users values('user','user','ROLE_USER',true);
```

3. Deploy the application to get the home page. On clicking the **Add New Contact** link, we will get the login form. If the credentials for role `admin` are entered as `admin - admin` for username and password, we will get the contact form.

4. If the credentials are wrong but the username is correct, we will get the following screen:

5. If we enter credentials for the user role as `user - user`, we will get an access denied page as follows:

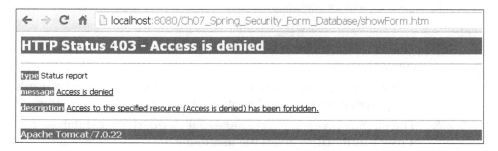

Case 4 – Remember me

Some of the URLs from the applications need to be secure but from the developer's point of view. The user never likes to get prompted to enter the credentials every time. We can have a `remember me` functionality, which lets the user keep users' information stored so that next time they don't have to authenticate themselves again. In order to provide the `remember me` functionality, we need to do the following steps:

1. Add a `remember me` tag under `<http>`, which provides the "remember me" functionality. The updated configuration will be as follows:

```
<security:http auto-config="true">
  <security:intercept-url pattern="/showForm.htm"
    access="ROLE_ADMIN"/>
  <security:form-login login-processing-url="/j_spring_security_
check"
    login-page="/login.jsp" default-target-url="/index.jsp"
    authentication-failure-url="/login.jsp?error=error"/>
  <security:remember-me key="contactdata"
    token-validity-seconds="2419200"/>
</security:http>
```

The `remember me` configuration takes two attributes, `key` and `token-validity-seconds`. This functionality works on the principle of cookie management. Whenever a user selects remember me, a cookie gets stored on the client machine which by default stores the value of username, password, expiry date, and a private key in MD5 encoded format. By default, the value of the private key is `SpringSecured` and this cookie exists for two weeks. In the above configuration, we made the private key `contactdata` which is application specific and it lasts for four weeks which we specified in seconds.

2. We need to update the login form as well as add Remember me as a checkbox, which has the action as `_spring_security_remember_me`. The code for it will be:

```
<tr><td><input id="remember_me"
          name="_spring_security_remember_me" type="checkbox"
/></td>
      <td><label for="remember_me">Remember me</label>
</td>
</tr>
```

3. On executing the application, when we click on the **Add new contact** link, we will get a login page with remember me functionality as follows:

4. On entering the correct credentials as admin - admin and on selecting the **Remember me** checkbox, we will get the contact form.

5. The next time we execute the same application and click on the **Add new contact** link, we will not get the login form but, in turn, the contact form will be directly given to us. This is because we selected the checkbox.

6. For further information on how it happens, we can check out cookie information from the browser after executing it on the Google browser. We can get it from cookie management as follows:

From the preceding diagram we can find out the date of cookie creation and expiry.

Case 5 – Logout

Once the authentication process is done, the user will be able to browse freely to access the data from the Web; login recognizes the user. In the same way, when a user completes the work, the user needs to log out so as to not leave his information open for browsing. To provide a logout mechanism, we need to perform the following two steps:

- Provide a link to log out
- Configure logout in `spring-security.xml` to redirect the user to the page which can be publicly accessible

Let's implement it in our application with the help of the following changes:

1. In the `header.jsp` file, add a Logout link as follows:

```
<a href="<c:url value='j_spring_security_logout'/>" style="font-size: large; font-family: Times New Roman; font: bold;"> Logout</a>
```

2. In `<http>`, configure the `<logout>` as:

```
<security:logout invalidate-session="true"
    logout-success-url="/index.jsp"/>
```

The preceding configuration tells the framework to redirect to `index.jsp` page on logout and invalidate the session so the information will be accessible after logout. We are set to check the logout functionality in our application. Now we will have Logout as a link on every page as shown in the following screenshot:

Way 2 – Spring Security using AOP

In the security method, we provide access restrictions to invoke a method rather than a URL. To enable annotation-based security in an application, we declare:

```
<global-method-security pre-post-annotations="enabled" use-
expression="true"/>
```

The preceding configuration enables us to use @Secured annotation in our Java code which takes a role name or expression. Spring supports the following four ways to secure methods:

- Annotating the method with @Secured

- Annotating the methods with @RolesAllowed

- Methods annotated with pre- and post-invocation annotations as @PreAuthorize, @PostAuthorize, @PostFilter, and @PreFilter

- Methods matched with pointcut expressions

The following configuration shows the use of expressions while securing a URL:

```
<security:intercept-urlpattern="/showForm.htm"
      access="hasRole('ROLE_ADMIN')"/>
```

The access attribute take the following values:

Expression	Return value
permitAll	Always true
denyAll	Always false
hasRole(role)	True if user has a specified role
hasAnyRole(role1,role2,.....)	True if user has one of the specified roles

@Secured

@Secured takes an array of string as an argument where each argument is a value of authorization, one of the roles the user should have to access the method. The Spring Security exception will be thrown whenever an unauthorized user tries to access the method.

@RolesAllowed

@RolesAllowed has been defined by JSR 250. To enable the annotation, we need to do the following configuration:

```
<global-method-security jsr250-annotations="enabled"/>
```

SpEL-enabled security annotations for securing the methods

Spring 3.0 has introduced four methods to secure the method invocation depending upon the role access, which are as follows:

- @PreAuthorized: The annotation takes the argument whose value will be the value of Role which can access the method as:

```
@PreAuthorized ("hasRole('ROLE_ADMIN')")
public int getData()
{
  //some code here
}
```

The method getData() can be accessed by the user who has the privilege as ROLE_ADMIN. Some expressions which we can use are as follows:

Sr.No	Expression	Description
1	hasRole(role)	The method checks for the role which has been passed as an argument and return true if the current principle has a specified role
2	hasAnyRole([role1,role2])	The method checks for any of the roles which have been passed roles separated by comma as an argument and returns true if the current principal has any of those supplied
3	Principal	This allows direct access to the principal object representing the current user
4	permitAll	This always evaluates to true as it permits all the users
5	denyAll	This always evaluates to false and not allowing anyone to access
6	isRememberMe()	The method returns true if the current principal is a remember me user
7	isAuthenticated()	The method returns true if the user is not anonymous
8	isFullyAuthenticated()	This returns true if the user is not an anonymous or a remember me user

@PostAuthorized: This annotation involves decision making, depending upon the object returned from the secured method:

```
@PostAuthorized("return Object.contact.email==principal.email")
public Contact getContact(String email)
{
  //some code here
}
```

The preceding configuration gives access to the user who has principal mail ID matched to the contact object returned from the function. Opposite to the @PreAuthorized annotation in @PostAuthorized, the method gets invoked first. So the method should not give any side effects if authorization fails.

- @PostFilter: In some situations, developers don't want to secure the method but want to secure the data returned from the method.

Let's implement method level security in our JdbcTemplate application, which we developed in cases 1 and 2 for URL-based security:

1. Add configuration to add method level security using an expression in the spring-security.xml file as follows:

   ```
   <security:global-method-security  secured-annotations="enabled"/>
   ```

2. By default, developers configure an access attribute which accepts a role name which can access the URL with correct authentication. But if the developer wants to use expressions as a user with some role (e.g. hasRole('admin')) or IP address (for example, hasIpAddress('123.123.1.1')) then we need to add use-expression="true" in <http>. We have already seen the expressions which can be used for configuration.

3. Let's configure access for the resources as:

   ° A home page to be available to all the users by configuring access='permitAll'

   ° showForm.htm to be accessed by the user having the role ROLE_ADMIN

   To do the preceding configurations, we need to update the <http> configuration as follows:

   ```
   <security:http auto-config="true"use-expressions="true">
       <security:intercept-url pattern="/index.jsp"
         access="permitAll"/>
       <security:form-login login-processing-url="/j_spring_security_
   check"
           login-page="/login.jsp"default-target-url="/index.jsp"
   ```

```
        authentication-failure-url="/login.jsp?error=error"/>
      <security:remember-me key="contactdata"
        token-validity-seconds="2419200"/>
    </security:http>
```

4. Use `@Secured('hasRole(ROLE_ADMIN')')` or `@Secured("ROLE_ADMIN')` on the `showContactForm()` method as we don't want everyone to access it. This will allow users with the `ROLE_ADMIN` privilege to access the functionality. The code will be as follows:

```
@Secured("ROLE_ADMIN")
  @RequestMapping("/showForm.htm")
  public ModelAndView showContactForm(HttpServletRequest request,
      HttpServletResponse response, ModelMap map) throws Exception
{

    Contact contact = new Contact();
    map.addAttribute(contact);
    return new ModelAndView("contactForm");
  }
```

5. We need to add the `aopalliance.jar` file as method security uses `Spring-AOP` internally. You can download it from `java2s.com` or `mvnrepository.com`.

6. Deploy the application and enter the credentials to check how the application is working.

Spring Security using pointcut

Sometimes in the application, more than one method needs to be secured. Putting constraints on the one-by-one method will not be good practice. In such cases, authorization can be applied using point cut. To use `pointcut` for securing methods, we need to configure `<protect-pointcut>` as follows:

```
<global-method-security>
<protect-pointcut access="ROLE_ADMIN"expression=
"execution(* com.packt.ch07.*.showContactForm(*))"/>
</global-method-security>
```

The preceding configuration restricts the access to `showContactForm` to the users who have the `ADMIN` role.

Way 3 – Custom security

Spring supports and provides all kinds of possible security methodologies, but then also, sometimes for certain situations, we need to provide our own custom way to extend spring API. One of the ways to provide custom security is by writing user-defined `AuthenticationProvider` which has the `authenticate()` method. This method uses `UserDetailService` to do authentication. The `authenticate()` method returns `AuthenticationToken` containing username, password, and authorities.

Summary

Security is a very important part of any application and needs to be carefully handled. As each application and its requirements are different due to the ways of authentication, like form-based or basic; the developers need to wisely make a decision on which one to use. In this chapter, we have seen URL-based, as well as method-based, ways to provide security. The users with their assigned roles can be configured in the XML. We also saw how to use databases to configure the authentication information. Sometimes the user uses the application frequently and may not want to log in each time they access the application. We also covered remember me functionality to take away the burden of login. We also saw how to use logout in the application.

In the next chapter, we will be covering problems during the versioning of an application, problems for collaborating on the application when it's been distributed among the team members. We will also configure the software which provides versioning and collaboration with ease.

8
Versioning and Deploying

We have made a great effort to create an application. As the application was quite simple and we were working alone on it, we haven't faced the difficulty of collaborating with each other. We never even came across a situation where the code had conflicts because someone else in the team did the changes. But in actual development, we always work in a team, no matter what the size. A team always works faster for better performance but faces problems when collaborating on the work, synchronizing with each other, when more than one person works on the same code, and many more. These are not code-related problems. Rather, the problem is how efficiently we exchange code with each one of our team members with less duplication. Versioning tools help us in such scenarios, as already discussed in the introductory chapter. In this chapter, we will explore the real power of **TortoiseSVN** as a versioning tool and how we can use it for collaboration. We will cover the following topics:

- How to use versioning to collaborate the code
- How to manage the application lifecycle
- How to use Tomcat for deploying an application

Versioning

In the introductory chapter, we already discussed what versioning is, why developers need versioning, and how to share the work in the repositories. We covered most of the basics which we implement practically in the coming pages. To start with versioning, we first need the TortoiseSVN setup and a server to manage TortoiseSVN. We do have servers such as the **VisualSVN** server, **Collabnet** server, and **UberSVN**.

First of all, we need to install TortoiseSVN. Let's perform the following steps to complete the installation:

1. Download the TortoiseSVN setup from `https://tortoisesvn.net/ downloads.html` for your platform.

2. Before starting the installation, configure the `JAVA_HOME` and `Path` variables.

3. Start the installation by clicking on the **Run** button.

4. A welcome screen will appear; click on **Next** to follow the step.

5. Then, accept the license agreement.

6. On the next screen, deselect the elements to start with custom setup. After selecting the elements to install, click on the **Next** button.

7. Click on **Install**.

8. Click on **Finish** to complete the setup.

Now it's time to install the server to maintain repositories, users, and much more.

Collabnet server

We will install Collabnet and Visual SVN as two different servers for this purpose. Let's start with Collabnet Subversion Edge. The setup is available at `http://www. collab.net/downloads/subversion`. Once the setup is downloaded, install it by keeping all the default settings.

We have installed the Collabnet server successfully. Now we will create repositories, and users, and assign the access rules to the repositories. Let's then start with repository creation:

1. From the **Start** menu, select **Collabnet** to launch it. We will get the console status as shown in the following screenshot:

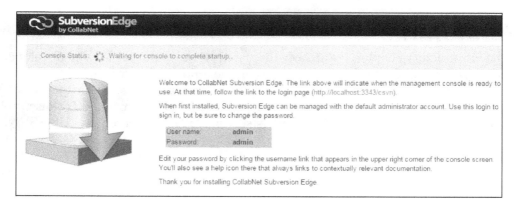

2. Once the setup is done, we will be prompted to provide authentication details as shown in the following snapshot:

Use admin as username and admin as password to log in.

3. We will get the home page. The server is down. We need to start it before any other function. To start it, click on the **Start** button as shown in the following screenshot:

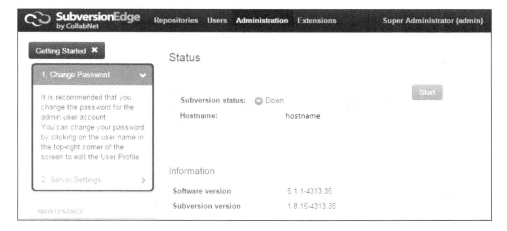

4. Once the server is on, now it's time to create the repository. Click on the **Repositories** menu, as shown here:

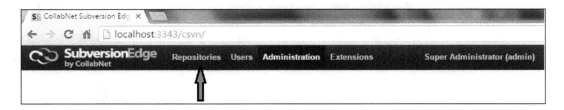

5. We will get the list of repositories if you have any, as shown here:

6. Click on the **Create** button to create a new repository.

7. We will get a form to enter the name of a new repository. Enter `Repository1` as shown in the following screenshot:

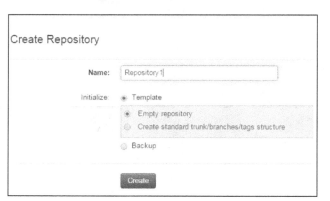

8. Once a successful repository gets created, we will get it in the list of repositories as we did in **step 2**. In this way, we can create many repositories.

9. Now let us create users. Click on **Users** from the menu bar as shown in the following screenshot:

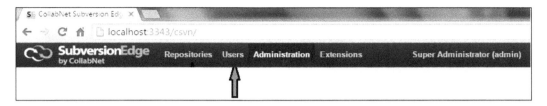

10. We will get a list of available users. We haven't created any users yet; we will get just admin as an available user as shown in the following screenshot:

We can even get the users list from the **User List** menu from the left panel as shown:

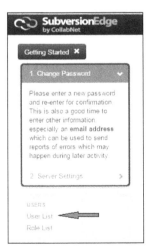

11. Let's add two more users here. Click on the **Create** button to get the create new user template as follows:

12. Add packt_user1 as **Login Name**, Contact1 as the password, select ROLE_USER as the role. Click on **create** to create a new user.

13. In the same way, create one more user with the username packt_user2 and password Contact1. You can use your choice of password but if you are using anything else please remember it as we need it in the future.

14. On clicking **User List**, we can get the user list with three users; admin, packt_user1, and packt_user2 as shown in the following screenshot:

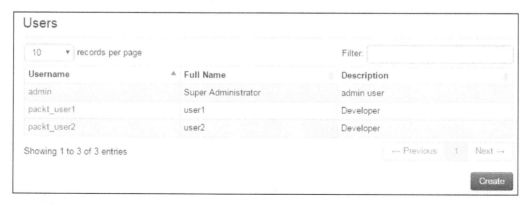

Next, let us see how to set access rules.

Repository1 should be accessed only by packt_user1 and packt_user2. To do this, we need to set access rules with the help of the following steps:

1. Click on the **Repositories** menu.

2. On the left panel, we will get **Access Rules** as shown in following screenshot:

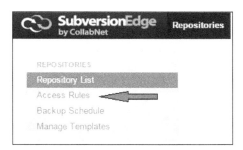

3. Click on **Access Rules**. As there are no rules set yet, all the users will be able to read and write to all the repositories. It can be seen as follows:

4. To set the rule, click on the **Edit** button and add new rules as shown in the following screenshot to give read and write access to both users which we have created:

Now we have successfully secured our repository so that only authenticated users will be able to access it.

Visual SVN server

It's time to create new users with the help of the following steps in Visual SVN.

Get the setup Visual SVN from `https://www.visualsvn.com/downloads/` and complete the setup with default settings.

1. Let's start the Windows-based VisualSVN server and explore its power to manage repositories.

2. Start the VisualSVN server from the **Start** menu. We will get the following window:

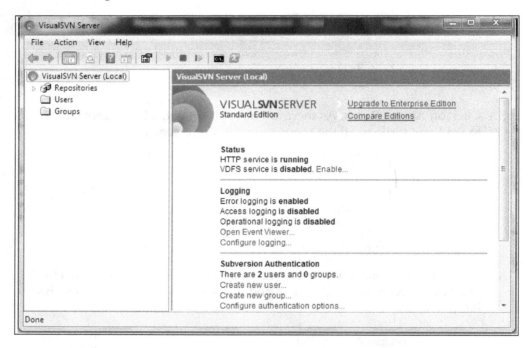

3. Now there are no repositories or users. We will now add them one by one. A new repository can be created in two ways:

    1. Right-click on the **Repositories** folder and select the **Create New Repository...** option:

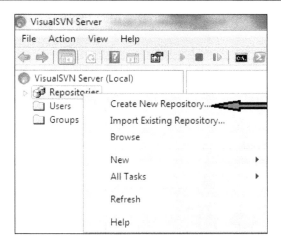

2. Click on **Create new repository** from the home page as shown in the following screenshot:

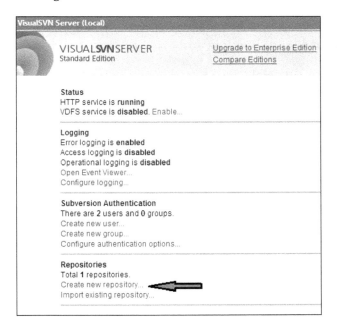

4. Select the default option to create **Regular FSFS repository** and click on **Next**:

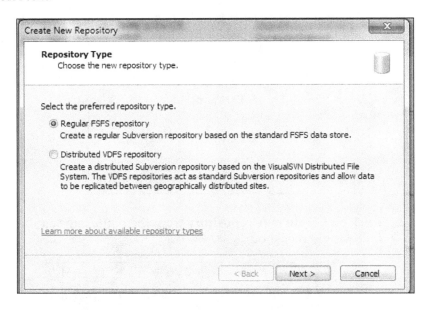

5. Give the repository the name `visual_repo1` and click on **Next** as shown in the following screenshot:

6. Select **Empty repository** and click on **Next** as shown:

7. Select **Custom permissions** and click on the **Custom** button to set access rules if we have users already created. As there are no users, we cannot set access rules now, we will set access rules in the following steps. Select **All Subversion users have read and write access** and click on **Create**:

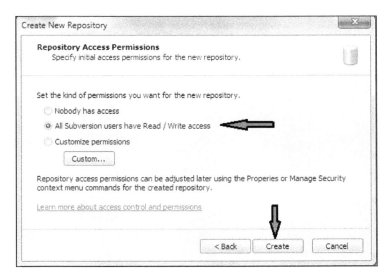

8. We will get a success page giving details like the name of the repository, the users who can access it, and the URL to be used to fetch the data as shown:

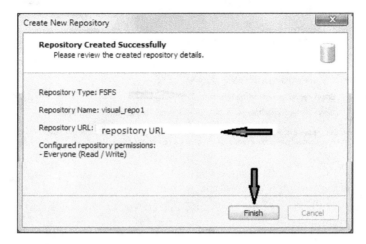

9. Click on **Finish** to complete the process. We will use this URL to perform an import of the repository or committing data to the repository.

We can now find our repository by clicking on **Repositories** on the left panel:

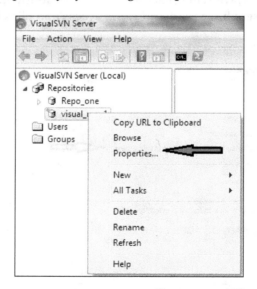

Now let us start creating users. A new user can be created in two ways:

1. Right-click on the Users folder and select the **Create User** option:

2. Click on **Create new user** from the home page as shown:

3. Fill the details in the form and click on **OK**. Use the username `svn_user1` and password `svnpass1`:

4. In the same way, add one more user having `svn_user2` as the username and `svnpass2` as the password.

5. On clicking **Users** in the left panel, we can get list of available users, as shown:

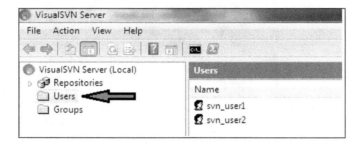

Next, we will add access rules for our repositories by performing the following steps:

1. Right-click `visual-repo1` and select the **Properties** option. Earlier, we created a repository without any access rules, all users can access that repository, hence we get the following screenshot:

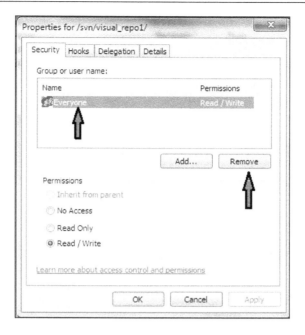

2. Select **Everyone** as shown in the preceding screenshot and click on **Remove**. Now no one can access `visual_repo1`.

3. Click on **Add** to add the new users which we created. We will get the following screenshot:

4. Select **svn_user1** and click on **OK**.

5. We will now get a properties dialog where **svn_user1** got added. Here we can set permissions by selecting the radio buttons. We will keep **Read / Write** but if you want you can change it here.

6. Add one more user, **svn_user2**, in the same way with read/write access. We will get a dialog as follows:

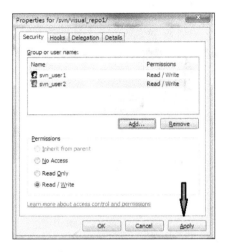

7. Click on **Apply** and then **OK** to reflect the changes.

Adding SVN as a plugin to Eclipse

Now, we can use TortoiseSVN through the command line. We don't have to keep on remembering all the commands to use versioning. As we are using Eclipse, we can use an SVN plugin to use versioning from our eclipse IDE. Let's integrate the SVN plugin as follows:

1. Select **Eclipse Marketplace** from the **Help** menu.

2. Type Subclipse in **Find** and click on **Search**.

3. Once the search gets completed, we will get **Subclipse** at the top of the list. Click on the **Install** button next to it as shown:

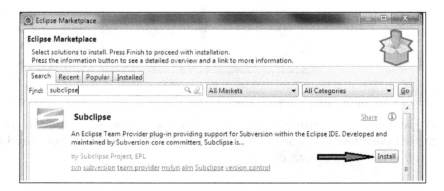

4. Select all the checkboxes to download the plugin as shown in the following screenshot:

5. Click on **Next**.

6. Select the **Accept the terms and condition** radio button.

7. Click on **Finish**.

8. A security warning will be shown; click on **OK** to proceed further.

9. Once installation is complete, we will get a dialog to restart eclipse as follows:

10. Click on **Yes** to restart.

We have successfully installed the plugin. We can check it by navigating to **Windows | Show View | other |**. Type svn. We should get the following screen:

Now we are set to start with versioning using eclipse. We will do it first with Collabnet and then with Visual SVN. To start with, we need to create two workspaces, svn_tut and svn_tut1, used by packt_user1 and packt_user2 respectively. Either we can get the project from the repository or if it's a new project, we can create a directory structure of it and commit it to the repository. In our repository, no projects are available; so now packt_user1 will create a new project and store it in the central repository **Repository1** so that others can access it from his or her group. Let's follow the steps to complete the task:

1. Launch eclipse and select the workspace **svn_tut1**.
2. Create a new dynamic web project SVNDemo1.
3. Right-click on it and select the option **Team | Share project**.
4. Select **SVN** and click on **Next** as shown:

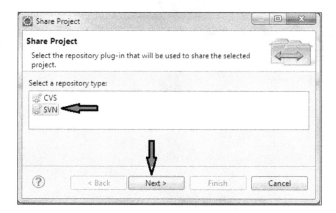

5. We now need to select the repository location. To enter the URL, select the **Create new repository location** radio button and click on **Next** as follows:

6. Enter the URL of `Repository1` from the Collabnet server. To find out the URL:

   ° Launch the Collabnet server.

   ° Enter the credentials.

   ° Click on **Repositories**; we will get the following screen, from where the red underlined part is the URL to enter:

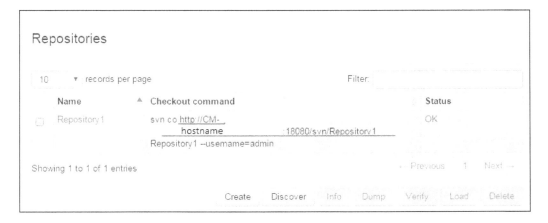

7. Copy and paste it in eclipse as repository info. Make sure to remove extra spaces from the URL. Click on **Next**:

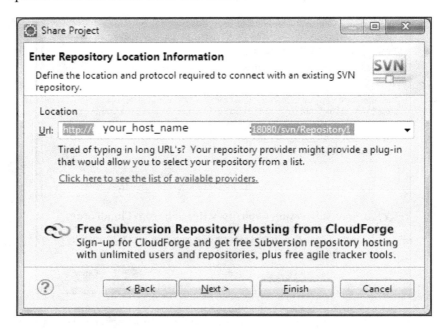

8. Select the project name as the folder name and click on **Next**.

9. Add comments as Initial Import and click on **Finish**.

10. We will be prompted to enter authentication several times. Use the credentials which we created while configuring the Collabnet server for `Repository1` (`packt_user1` as username and `contact1` as password).

11. Once the operation is completed, we will be prompted to open Perspective. Click on **No**.

12. Now we have to commit the project to the repository. To do this, right-click on **Project**, select **Team** and click on **Commit**.

13. Enter the comments as **Empty project**; we can deselect the checkboxes for the files which we don't want to add for versioning. Now we will keep everything default as shown in the following screenshot:

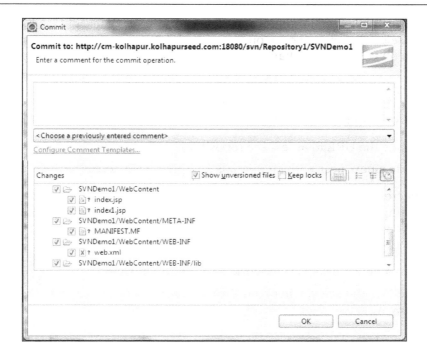

Adding files in the project and committing them to the repository

After creating our project, now it's time to add packages or files:

1. Let's add `index.jsp` in `WebContent`.

2. The newly created file will have ? as an icon signifying this is new content which is not added to versioning as shown in the following screenshot:

3. To add this in versioning, we need to commit this file. Right click on **index. jsp**, select **Team**, and click on **Commit**. Add the appropriate comment and click on **OK**. The files have been successfully committed to the repository.

Importing the project in the workspace

To get the project in the workspace, first of all the repository administrator has to:

- Give us the URL to access the repository
- Create a new user with credentials and give them access to the repository

We already created `packt_user2`, who has access to `Repository1`. We will use this data to import the project from the repository. The process is generally called checkout. We will follow the following steps to check out the `SVNDemo1` project from `Repository1`:

1. Open a new workspace to work. Select **File | Import**.

2. Type `SVN` and select **Checkout Projects from SVN** as shown in the following screenshot:

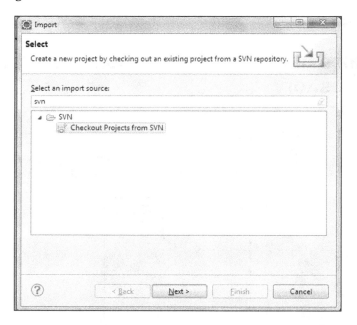

3. Click on **Next**. Select **Create a new repository location** and click on **Next**.

4. Enter the URL of the repository which you got from the administrator or copied from Collabnet as shown earlier.

5. Enter the credentials as `packt_user2` and `Contact1` or the one which you gave at the time of user creation.

6. All the projects from `Repository1` will be listed as shown in the following screenshot:

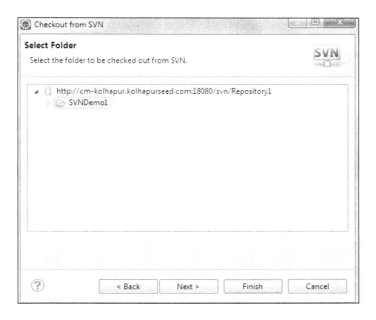

7. Select **SVNDemo1** and click on **Next**. Enter credentials if asked.

8. Choose **Check out as a project in the workspace** as shown in the following screenshot:

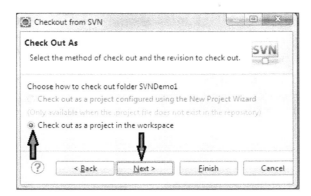

9. Click on **Next**.

10. Select **Use Default work location** and click on **Finish**.

11. We have successfully checked out the project from the repository. It is a replica of the project which `packt_user1` had committed.

12. Let's modify `index.jsp` and commit it to understand the concept of collaboration:

    1. Modify `index.jsp` as follows:

    ```
    <body>
    WELCOME to Collabnet.
    <body>
    ```

    2. A black star will be shown on `index.jsp`, signifying we made some changes in the local file which we can commit to the repository as shown:

    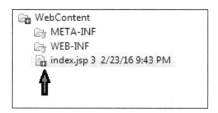

    3. Right click on `index.jsp`, select **Team** and click on **Commit**.

    4. Enter a comment as `Welcome message` and click on **OK**. The file will be committed to the repository.

Updating and tracking the project for latest changes in the repository

As project development is a team effort, many people may be working on different files in the project. That means they will keep on committing their latest work to the repository. In order to reflect those changes in our local copy, we must update our project. `packt_user2` has added `index.jsp` in the last step, which is not with `packt_user1`.

Let's update the project for `packt_user1` to get the latest copy with the help of the following steps:

1. First of all, we may want to find out what changes have been made in the `SVNDemo1` project. To find this out, right click on **projectSVNDemo1 | Team | Synchronize with Repository**.

2. Enter the credentials for `packt_user1`. We will be prompted to open Perspective. Click on **Yes**.

3. In Perspective, we will get a list of the files which are in the repository but not in our local copy as shown in the following screenshot:

4. Now we will accept all the changes from the repository in our local copy as:

    5. Change Perspective to get the project explorer.

    6. Right-click on **WebContent**, select **Team**, and click on **Update to Head**.

    7. Enter `packt_user1`'s credentials.

    8. We will now have `index.jsp` with the same code added by `packt_user2` in the previous steps.

5. To find the version history, we need to click on **project->Team->Show History**. A dialog will open as shown, with the list of the operations performed on the project to keep a history of versioning:

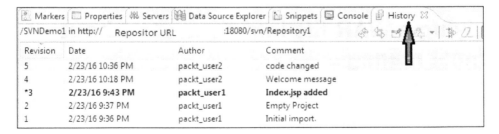

In the same way we used Collabnet for versioning, we can use a VisualSVN server. The only difference is the way we copy the URL. To copy the URL for the repository in VisualSVN, we need to right-click on the repositories and select **Copy URL to the Clipboard** as shown in the following screenshot:

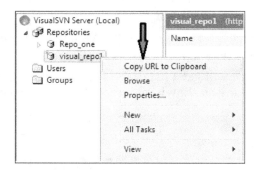

Use the same step to check out, add, and update the data to and from the repository **visual-repo1** which we have already created. Follow the same steps as we did for Collabnet. Don't forget to check the credentials for the VisualSVN server.

Project deployment

We created the project in Eclipse IDE and tested it there. It may be possible to give our project to others to use, or want to use it on some other machine. The process of installing our application into the server context is called **project deployment**. This process is server-specific. On successful deployment, we can use a project without eclipse IDE. Here we will discuss the possible ways of deploying our application into a Tomcat7 server.

We can create a **web archive file (WAR)** and deploy it in Tomcat with one of the two ways described in the following sections.

Copying a WAR file into Tomcat without Tomcat manager

To copy a WAR file of our application, first of all we need to generate the WAR file from eclipse as follows:

1. Create a new dynamic web project, Ch08_Demo_Deployment.

2. Add index.jsp in WebContent as follows:

```
<%@page language="java" contentType="text/html; charset=ISO-8859-1"
pageEncoding="ISO-8859-1"%>
```

```
<!DOCTYPE html PUBLIC"-//W3C//DTD HTML 4.01 Transitional//
EN""http://www.w3.org/TR/html4/loose.dtd">
<html>
<head>
<meta http-equiv="Content-Type" content="text/html;
charset=ISO-8859-1">
<title>Insert title here</title>
</head>
<body>
Welcome to Project
<a href="welcome.jsp">CLICK HERE</a>
</body>
</html>
```

3. Add `welcome.jsp` in `WebContent` as follows:

```
<%@page language="java"content Type="text/html; charset=ISO-8859-1"
pageEncoding="ISO-8859-1"%>
<!DOCTYPE html PUBLIC"-//W3C//DTD HTML 4.01 Transitional//
EN""http://www.w3.org/TR/html4/loose.dtd">
<html>
<head>
<meta http-equiv="Content-Type" content="text/html;
charset=ISO-8859-1">
<title>Insert title here</title>
</head>
<body>
Hello from Tomcat
</body>
```

4. Let's now generate a **WAR file** by right-clicking on **project | Export | WAR file** as shown:

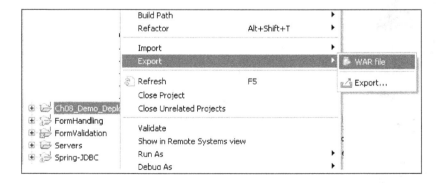

5. Click on **Browse** to select the destination, for example, **C** drive or any other location.

6. Enter the filename as `MyProject1` and click on **Save**.

7. Open the Tomcat installation directory from the drive and browse to `webapps`.

8. Copy **MyProject1.war** in **webapps** as shown in the following screenshot:

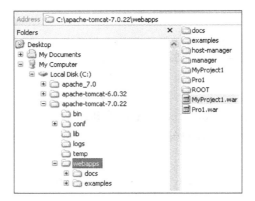

9. To check the project is working, perform the following steps:

    1. Browse to `tomcat-> bin` and start the Tomcat server by double-clicking on the startup batch file.

    2. Once Tomcat is started, we can observe the following log on the **Tomcat** console, where Tomcat got started at `8080` and our WAR got deployed as shown:

```
Tomcat
INFO: Initialization processed in 918 ms
Mar 3, 2016 8:20:29 AM org.apache.catalina.core.StandardService startInternal
INFO: Starting service Catalina
Mar 3, 2016 8:20:29 AM org.apache.catalina.core.StandardEngine startInternal
INFO: Starting Servlet Engine: Apache Tomcat/7.0.22
Mar 3, 2016 8:20:29 AM org.apache.catalina.startup.HostConfig deployWAR
INFO: Deploying web application archive MyProject1.war
Mar 3, 2016 8:20:29 AM org.apache.catalina.startup.HostConfig deployDirectory
INFO: Deploying web application directory docs
Mar 3, 2016 8:20:29 AM org.apache.catalina.startup.HostConfig deployDirectory
INFO: Deploying web application directory examples
Mar 3, 2016 8:20:29 AM org.apache.catalina.startup.HostConfig deployDirectory
INFO: Deploying web application directory host-manager
Mar 3, 2016 8:20:29 AM org.apache.catalina.startup.HostConfig deployDirectory
INFO: Deploying web application directory manager
Mar 3, 2016 8:20:30 AM org.apache.catalina.startup.HostConfig deployDirectory
INFO: Deploying web application directory ROOT
Mar 3, 2016 8:20:30 AM org.apache.coyote.AbstractProtocol start
INFO: Starting ProtocolHandler ["http-apr-8080"]
Mar 3, 2016 8:20:30 AM org.apache.coyote.AbstractProtocol start
INFO: Starting ProtocolHandler ["ajp-apr-8009"]
Mar 3, 2016 8:20:30 AM org.apache.catalina.startup.Catalina start
INFO: Server startup in 742 ms
```

3. Open the browser and write the URL for our project, which is `http://localhost:8080/MyProject1` in the format of `http://host_name:port_no/Name_of_war`.

4. We will get the following output from the index page:

5. When we click on the link, the welcome page will go on browsing through the project.

With the help of the preceding steps, we can deploy any project we have created in this project without any extra effort apart from configuring security, as security users need to be created in the server's configuration.

Copying a WAR file into Tomcat with Tomcat manager

To deploy a WAR using Tomcat manager, we first need to have a user who has a manager role. So let's first of all create a user with a managerial role:

1. Stop Tomcat if already running. Open the `webapps` folder and delete `MyProject1.war` and the `MyProject` folder from it. We will now deploy it with a new process.

2. Open `tomcat-users.xml` from the `tomcat | conf` folder.

3. Edit it to add a role as `manager-gui` and a user with `tomcat` as username and `tomcat` as password. The code will be as follows:

```
<role rolenam'e="manager-gui"/>
<user username="tomcat" password="tomcat" roles="manager-gui"/>
```

4. Start Tomcat and type the following URL in the browser:
`http://localhost:8080/manager`.

5. It will ask for authentication. Enter `tomcat` as username and password as `tomcat`, which we have just given in the earlier step.

6. A page for the Tomcat web application manager will open. We will get a deployment form as follows:

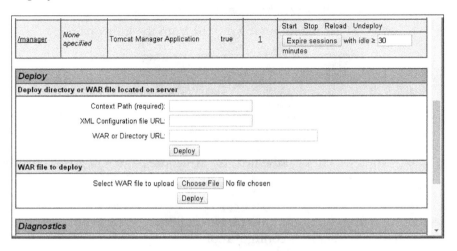

7. Click on **Choose File** and select **MyProject1.war** from the destination which we exported in a previous step.

8. Click on **Deploy**.

9. We will be able to find **/MyProject1** in the **Application** list as follows:

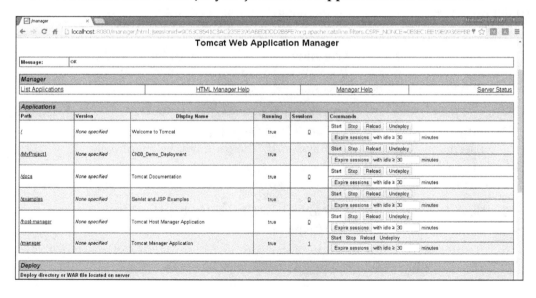

10. Test it from the browser in the same way as we did in a previous step by typing the URL.

In this way, we can deploy a WAR of any project which we have created in the Tomcat environment.

Summary

In this chapter, we discussed how to configure a Collabnet server and a Visual SVN server. We covered the creation of users and repositories in both the servers. We also set the access rules to the repositories. We learned the integration of the **Subclipse** plugin in Eclipse to do versioning of projects from IDE. In easy steps, we discovered the process of collaborating on the project with team members, with the help of commit and update commands. We also covered the process of getting a new project in our workspace from the repository to work. Deployment is one of the very important steps in application development. We covered deployment of applications with and without Tomcat Manager. And with this, now you are set to get on with your own application development.

We started the journey by taking a simple application and develop it step-by-step. We practically discovered the ways to develop modular Java programming using SpringMVC. We developed a contact management application layer by layer to make it easy to understand and develop thoroughly. Developing an application which contains no flaws in business logic is possible if we carry out unit testing and integration testing. Unsecure applications will not withstand the market so we make sure our application is secure by using integration with Spring Security. The messy work of handling teamwork has been made easy with the help of versioning. Once the application was ready, we performed the deployment of the application on the server, which was our last stop. I have tried to make this journey as smooth as possible. Hope you enjoyed it and will explore it further.

Index

A

annotation-based validations
@Length(min=, max=) 62
@Max 62
@Min 62
@NotBlank 62
@NotEmpty 62
@NotNull 62
@Pattern(regex=, flag= 63
@Size(min=, max=) 63
@Valid 63
performing 59-65
Arquillian 146
Aspect Oriented Programming (AOP) 114

B

branching 14
business layer
developing 107-111
business logic
about 104-106
business layer, developing 107-111
case studies 107
conditions 107
domain knowledge 106
formulas 107
rules 107

C

client program 16
cohesive 3
Collabnet server 173
Collabnet Subversion Edge
download link 174

command object 47
committing 16
Concurrent Versioning System (CVS) 14
container 12
coupling 3

D

data
saving in relational database,
advantages 69
storing in XML, disadvantages 68
data binding, presentation layer
about 43
multiple form fields, reading 46, 47
request parameters for searching,
reading 43-45
Data Source Name (DSN) 70
data sources
getting 77
getting by looking up, JNDI used 77
getting, from JDBC sources 78
declarative transaction 113
isolation level 115
managing, in Spring 114-117
propagation behavior 114
read-only 116
rollback rules 117
transaction-timeout 116
declarative transaction management 117-119
design patterns 10
development 2
distributed versioning
about 17
GitHub 17
domain knowledge 106

E

Eclipse
SVN, adding as plugin 188-192
enterprise
as an application 19, 20
Expression Language (EL) 51

F

filters
BasicAuthenticationFilter 154
DefaultLoginPageGeneratingFilte 154
LogoutFilter 154
UsernamePasswordAuthenticationFilter
155
form backing object 47
form validation, presentation layer
about 53
annotation-based validations 59
customised validators, developing with
Spring validators 54-59
framework
about 29
advantages 29, 30

G

GitHub 17
global transactions 112
Google
URL 42

H

Hibernate
about 86
architecture 87-93
Spring Hibernate integration 93-97

I

integration testing 133-141

J

Java
interacting, with relational database 69
Java Database Connectivity (JDBC)
about 69
and transaction management 112
issues 86
Java driver
advantages 73
disadvantages 73-76
Java EE platform
about 20
features 21
MVC I architecture 24
MVC II architecture 25
practical aspect 25-29
Servlet 23, 24
world of dotcoms 22
Java Enterprise architecture 11, 12
**Java Naming and Directory Interface
(JNDI) 77**
Java Transaction API (JTA) 112
JDBC drivers, types
about 70
Java driver 73
JDBC Net Protocol Driver 72
JDBC-ODBC bridge driver 70, 71
JDBC integration, types
about 78
DataSource, integrating to get connection
reference 79-81
JDBC DAO support, integrating 84, 85
JDBC template, integrating 82-84
**JDBC Native API Driver/Partly
JAVA Driver 71**
advantages 71
disadvantages 72
JDBC Net Protocol Driver
advantages 72
disadvantages 73
JDBC-ODBC bridge driver 70
advantages 70
disadvantages 71

L

local transactions 112

M

maintenance 2
Mockito testing
  about 141-146
  Arquillian 146
Mock testing
  about 127
  contact, inserting by violating validation
      rules for contacts 130-133
  contact, inserting with correct values as
      per validation rules 128-130
  Spring testing framework 127
modular programming
  about 4
  world of modules 4
modules
  about 3
  practical aspect 3
modules, for handling Spring Security
  ACL 151
  CAS Client 151
  configuration 151
  Core 152
  LDAP 152
  OpenID 152
  Web 152
multiple form fields
  form backing object 47-49
  multiple form fields, reading 47
  pre-population of forms 50-53

N

N-tier applications 9, 10

O

object-oriented programming (OOP)
      language 69
Object Relational Mapping (ORM)
  about 86
  advantages 86

object serialization
  disadvantages 68
One-tier application 7
Open Database Connectivity (ODBC)
      API 70

P

persistence
  about 67
  data, saving in relational database 68
  data, storing in XML 68
  object serialization, using 68
persistency 67
pre-population of forms 50
presentation layer
  about 41, 42
  data binding 43
  form validation 53
programmatic transaction management 113,
      119-121
project deployment
  about 198
  WAR file, copying into Tomcat without
      Tomcat manager 198-201
  WAR file, copying into Tomcat with
      Tomcat manager 201, 202

R

requirement collection phase 2

S

SCM (supply chain management) 14
Secure Service Layer (SSL) 152
security
  authentication 150
  authorization 150
  confidentiality 150
  data integrity 150
sequential programming language (SQL) 69
serialization 68
software application 1, 2
software development process models 2
software testing
  about 123, 124

spiral model 125
V model 125
waterfall model 124
SpEL enabled security annotations
@PostAuthorized 170
@PostFilter 170
@PreAuthorized 169
spiral model 125
Spring
and transaction management 112
Spring-JDBC integration
about 76
DataSource, configuring 77
Spring MVC
about 30
components 31
configuration file 33
front controller 32
ModelAndView 32
Spring MVC controller 32
ViewResolver 33
Spring Security for URL, using servlet filters
about 153-157
authentication against database 163, 164
basic authentication 157-160
login form authentication 161, 162
logout mechanism 167
remember me functionality 165, 166
Spring Security framework
about 151
custom security 172
secure web request 152
Servlet filters, using 151
SprAOP, using 168
Spring AOP, using 151
Spring Security for URL, using servlet
filters 153-157
Spring Security, using AOP
@RolesAllowed 168
@Secured 168about 168
pointcut, using 171
SpEL enabled security annotations for
securing methods 169-171
Spring testing framework 127
Spring validators
used, for developing customised
validators 54-59

Subversion (SVN)
about 4
architecture 15
repository 15, 16
SVN, adding as plugin to Eclipse
about 188-192
files, adding in project 193, 194
files, committing to repository 193
project, importing in workspace 194196
project, tracking for latest changes 196-198
project, updating for latest changes 196-198

T

team
coordinating with 13
three-tier applications 8
tier
about 5, 6
N-tier applications 9, 10
one-tier applications 7
three-tier applications 8
two-tier applications 7
TortoiseSVN 173
TortoiseSVN setup
download link 174
transaction management
about 111, 112
and JDBC 112
and Spring 112, 113
transaction, properties
about 111
atomicity 111
consistency 112
durability 112
isolation 112
two-tier applications 7

U

UberSVN 174
unit testing
about 98
JUnit used 98
TestCase writing, annotation used 98-102

V

versioning
    about 13, 173, 174
    collabnet server 174-179
versioning tools
    about 13
    Apache Subversion 14
    centralized versioning 14
visual SVN server
    about 180-187
    reference link 180
    SVN, adding as plugin to Eclipse 188-192
VisualSVN server 173
V model
    about 125
    validation phases 126, 127
    verification phases 126

W

waterfall model 124
web application
    security, providing 150, 151
web archive file (WAR) 198
work
    sharing 12, 13

www.ingramcontent.com/pod-product-compliance
Lightning Source LLC
Chambersburg PA
CBHW060552060326
40690CB00017B/3682